Using Scary Stories in the Classroom:

Lesson Plans, Activities and Curriculum Connections

Pamela Schembri

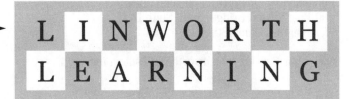

A Publication of Linworth Learning

Cataloging-in-Publication Data

Published by Linworth Publishing, Inc.
480 East Wilson Bridge Road, Suite L
Worthington, Ohio 43085

ISBN 1-58683-104-6

Table of Contents

Table of Contents continued

Table of Figures

How To Use This Book

Thrills and chills, witches, ghosts and goblins - these terrifying teaching tools may be a little controversial but they will surely inspire some of your most reluctant readers.

This book has a wide variety of spine-tingling activities and ideas, and was designed to guide teachers and librarians through the successful selection and use of more than 500 scary resources. You will learn how to use a child's natural fascination with things that go bump in the night to "scare" them into learning and loving to read.

Part One of the book offers practical tips to consider when choosing and presenting scary material, and when facing censorship and complaints from parents.

Part Two provides lesson plans and activities for classroom teachers and school or public librarians that are linked to language arts, social studies, science, math, technology and art curriculum.

Part Three is a comprehensive, annotated list of resources, including print and audiovisual materials, Web sites and highlights of selected scary stories. The recommended books are presented by category and type. As a professional storyteller and media specialist for eight years, the author has used these resources many times and knows their strengths. In composing this book, she has highlighted those strengths in the hope that even the most hesitant teacher will give this genre consideration. The resources included are instructional, enriching, appropriate and popular.

The carefully selected material in this book can be used in a number of ways. If interest is lagging in a particular subject area, add some spice with one of the suggested activities or use them as a starting point to integrate your favorite scary story into your lesson plans.

Using the brief book summaries in Part Three, choose an appropriate picture book to entice a reluctant reader. Learn how to turn Halloween into an irresistible celebration of reading and learning. The booktalks and tips for booktalking presented here can serve as an inspiration for you to create your own booktalks from your favorite tales of horror.

After reading more than 2,500 scary stories, the author came away with a full appreciation of the value and timeless appeal of a scary story. They can be terrifying, thought provoking, silly, chilling and even downright fun! Why not try one in your classroom today?

Warm Regards,

Marlene Woo-Lun
Publisher

Getting Started:
Practical
Techniques

Know Your Audience and Develop Objectives

Perhaps the best starting point when using scary stories is to evaluate your target audience and your accountability. Who will be using the materials? Why are you presenting scary stories to them? Is your population conservative or liberal? As a professional, you must make an honest assessment of your community and be prepared to delicately balance nervous adults with enthusiastic children.

Sometimes it is important to have objectives for presenting literature, especially if you work in a school. This can be tricky, however, because scary stories often don't have an objective; they have been told or written for the sheer enjoyment they bring. And for whatever reasons, enjoyment has failed to become a benchmark in most schools. Of course, as librarians, we know better. Enjoyable reading *is* education, and kids read and enjoy scary books.

To approach this situation, you can use the following objectives. They have been adapted from Gloria Treadwell Pipkin's defense concerning the text of censored literature (Karolides, Burress, & Kean, 112-113). Select the appropriate ones for your lesson, and add to the list when necessary.

Objectives for Using Scary Stories and Folktales

1. To explore historical and contemporary forces or attitudes that have influenced the culture of a society.

2. To motivate readers to examine their own attitudes and behaviors and to consider their rights and responsibilities.

3. To develop responses to the text and to examine reader interaction with the text.

4. To emphasize and develop the reader's active role in meaning-making.

5. To identify and assess the effectiveness of the author's technique.

6. To inspire further reading and writing.

Familiarize Yourself with the Resources

How do you start to sift through everything that can be considered scary? While I personally think ducks hanging from restaurant windows in Chinatown are scary, that's not the kind of literature I'm hoping to classify. In her book *Genreflecting: A Guide to Reading Interests in Genre Fiction*, Diana Herald subdivides horror fiction into numerous categories. Some of the more prevalent topics appropriate for this age level include ghost stories, cosmic paranoia, witches and warlocks, the occult and supernatural, haunted houses, monsters, vampires, animals running rampant, werewolves, and comic horror (Herald, 158). I have adapted these categories slightly to suit the younger K-6 audience.

Categories for Scary Resources

1. **Scary stories:** These resources for the very young deal with early fears (of the dark, of being alone) and the ability to overcome those fears. The titles of these books usually include the word *scary* (*Scary, Scary Halloween*).

2. **Ghost Stories:** These stories focus on restless spirits that travel the earth either seeking revenge or offering help.

3. **Haunted Houses:** These tales center on places where ghosts, goblins, or other supernatural beings inhabit.

4. **Stories of the Supernatural:** This category sums up anything unexplainable, such as a phantom hitchhiker or a funeral of the dead.

5. **Halloween Stories:** Again presented for the very young, these stories acquaint them with the cast of characters that may be lurking the streets disguised as trick-or-treaters.

6. **Monster Stories:** This category includes zombies, things unmentionable under the bed, mummies, werewolves, vampires, and more specifically, Frankenstein and Dracula. Take your pick.

7. **Witches:** Witches need their own category because they are the most prevalent evil figure in folklore. You'll find them in everything from Hansel and Gretel to stories of the Baba Yaga. Oddly enough, there had not been many wizard or warlock stories (prior to Harry Potter), but they would also fall into this subdivision.

8. **Funny stories:** These stories lead the reader to a scary place, then turn the tables to draw a laugh.

These categories give a sampling of the possibilities available to you. But the key to the successful presentation of scary stories lies in the knowledge of the material, not in the classification. In a sense, you have to get your hands dirty to confidently use scary stories, for the degree of fear varies greatly within a single category. The one invariable factor I have discovered when working with K-6 students is that the mood of fear is far more important than the actual gory details. When looking for good scary stories, I base my selections on the following criteria, which are a combination of standards adapted from Douglas Winter and my own personal taste (Kies, 10-12).

Criteria for Selecting Scary Stories

1. Is the story original?

I am always impressed when a writer can take a common scary folktale and give it a fresh retelling. A great example is Robert San Souci's story, "Lavender" (*Short and Shivery*), which is an elaborate version of the urban legend, "The Vanishing Hitchhiker."

2. Are the characters human and likable?

I look for characters that I can relate to, or even present as a real person. Sometimes I retell a story and mention that it happened to a relative, a close friend, or me. That's when I know I really like a story. I also avoid psychotic killers and madmen, in literature and real life.

3. Is the story reality-based, or is it a mystery that is not resolved?

"True" stories are the best, even if they never happened. These stories evoke questions that continue far beyond the library doors and spur children to share stories with others.

4. Does the story have just enough bad taste to make it scary?

Typically, people should not be exhuming bodies in search of gold or gems, but in scary stories they do it all the time!

5. Is the fear effectively suggested rather than graphically detailed?

Sure, we need to know that children were disappearing while the sausage maker was getting rich, but do we need to know the crunching sound an arm makes when placed in a high-powered grinder? Probably not.

6. Does the story create a lasting impression?

I have a hard time judging what makes a lasting impression these days. I think children are more desensitized than I am when it comes to considering something scary. Sometimes a story or an image lingers with me for days because I found it substantially disturbing, but I later find that students know that same story and are completely unimpressed. It's a learning process.

7. Do the characters find trouble because they broke the rules?

A theme that recurs in scary stories is that of the character who gets "what's coming." Originally these were, and still are, teaching tools used to warn children of the dangers of arrogance, ignorance and disobedience.

Preview Material

Certainly, no librarian has time to preview every title that is purchased, but in the case of horror material, you may need to. What one reviewer deems appropriate may be offensive to you or your population. The patrons who turn to you for guidance, whether in a school or public library, trust you to give them accurate information. Most children don't have an advanced censoring mechanism to stop them from indulging in the more graphic horror stories. Those who do voice their limitations often find themselves in great conflict with the rest of American society, which has been desensitized by the horror of everyday news.

Although you cannot determine what is too scary, you can share your thoughts with potential readers. They need to know.

It is always a good idea to make specific notes concerning the contents of books. I've done this for years with every chapter book, so that my addling mind doesn't embarrass me at work. I keep an index card file with short notes that I refer to each time I want to booktalk a title. Perhaps a book has nine wonderful stories and one clunker. Maybe passages need to be edited for some groups. I try to avoid promoting books to the wrong level of audience, and that takes some initial work.

Present the Material

Avoid a "Challenging" Situation: Techniques to Avoid Challenges

When sharing literature that may be considered even mildly scary, alert your listeners and offer them an alternative. In any audience, you may have children who, for religious or other reasons, cannot listen to or be part of the stories that make up horror literature. You may have students who scare easily, and hopefully you will be sensitive to their needs. I open each lesson with a few announcements, such as these.

Grades K-1: "Today, I have a great story to share with you, but it's a little scary. It has a witch in it." I immediately let the children know that something out of the ordinary may happen. Even by age five, children who belong to certain religions know that some things are not acceptable for their families, and they will tell you. Perhaps you can provide an alternative, such as a book on tape, for those students. I also let the listeners know that what I am sharing will not be too scary, so they feel safe and can enjoy the tale.

Grades 2-3: "I'm going to tell a scary story today." There will be applause, followed by, "Yeah! Tell us Freddy!" (as in Krueger, from the movie *A Nightmare on Elm Street*). How they

even know that name is a mystery to me. When the students are quiet again, I simply ask, "Is this going to be a problem for anyone, for any reason?" If a student looks timid, I may switch to a milder story, or perhaps to a funny story to gain trust. Again, knowing my audience and the material available beforehand gives me a good idea of what I can use.

Grades 4-6: With these students, I am much more direct. "Is anyone NOT able to listen to a story with a _____ (witch, devil, ghost) in it due to your religion?" I try to offer these students an alternate lesson without disrupting the main class. At this age level, I no longer announce that the story will be scary. I have found that when I do make this introduction, some students then vocally challenge each turn in the story as if to prove their lack of fear. Instead, I may say, "This story is a little spooky, but not too bad," and I draw the listeners into participation, not anticipation. Most students at this age do not scare easily, and some tell me that what I offer is not scary. Unfortunately, many parents allow their children to watch extremely violent or grotesque shows, so the students are, in a sense, dulled to horror that I find acceptable to use in the school setting. However, I am not thwarted, for my scary stories are in constant demand, and the students often ask for repeat storytellings.

As a presenter to children, you can safely assume that at some point something will go awry. Whether you are presenting the Preamble to the Constitution or a poem by Edgar Allan Poe, you must be visually alert during your presentation and monitor the situation as needed. I've had a few tangles in my work, but never anything serious.

I once had a second grade student "turn green" after hearing a spooky tale. Afterward, she confided that she was going to have nightmares. We had a discussion not only about the story but also about her options. Could she talk about the story with her classmates, family, or teacher? Did she want to leave the room if a scary story was told in the future? In the course of the talk, the student resolved her fears. The actual discussion took her mind from the visualization of the story back to reality.

Another situation took place at a public library when a parent insisted that her four-year-old child sit in with the ten-year-olds for a Halloween storytelling. I warned that the stories would not be suitable for young children, but, needless to say, my warning went unheeded. The tears that resulted from one tale could only be assuaged by a soothing apology and a quick turn to a humorous story. Because scary stories are so appealing, yet overwhelming at times, try to have a backup.

A Note About Censorship, Challenges, and Formal Complaints

Sometimes, even after the most careful planning and selection, a parent or administrator will object to your use of scary stories. You can't avoid this issue since you are dealing with somewhat controversial subject matter. Bear in mind that people have challenged everything from *Cinderella* to *The Bible*, so it stands to reason that you may incite some action when inviting children to consider the supernatural and undead.

Censors want to protect readers—all readers. Librarians promote the *Freedom to Read* for all. The two are on opposite ends of a spectrum, and righteousness on either side only denies eventual vision. Censorship is a fascinating issue, and it keeps you alert as a librarian. There are many great books that discuss the opposing viewpoints, but this is not one of them. What you need to know regarding censorship is this: scary stories top the lists of challenged materials in the United States. My favorite has been the challenge of *Scary Stories to Tell in the Dark*, once banned because it was "too scary." Challenges are a reality, and although they are often preventable, you need to be prepared.

When faced with a formal complaint, the best tool is a comprehensive written policy stating the criteria for selection. Selection, not censorship, is your framing guideline. If a book that you carry is formally challenged, there are steps to take. They are outlined in detail by the American Library Association, and resources can be found in Appendix A. Your policy, which is then adopted by your board, should include not only the criteria for selection but also a formal written procedure regarding challenges of controversial materials.

The formal process to remove a material from a collection is quite detailed. One of the earliest steps requires the potential censor to read, view, or listen to the work in its entirety and then complete a form detailing the exact nature of the offensive material. This step alone usually stops challengers in their tracks, but again, this is not what you hope for if you are a librarian working to establish good public relations.

Instead, when a parent or other person comes to you with an objection, I suggest you stop and listen. Talk informally about the options that can be taken to satisfy that person's viewpoint as well as your support of the Library Bill of Rights. I once read that a parent objected to a poem in Jack Prelutsky's *Nightmares* because her daughter, after hearing it, was so bothered that she suffered from stomachaches all night. While that's not terrible, if I were the librarian, I would apologize to the parent and child and perhaps revise my use of the poem. Maybe next time, I would give the poem a "grossness rating" as an introduction, or perhaps I would tell it in a humorous style. Of course, there's no pleasing everyone, which is why librarians discourage censorship, but there are plenty of materials to choose from. I simply experiment and adjust my program. It is a process that teaches me about people.

Perhaps an agreement can be made or an alternate assignment can be arranged. Ultimately the decision comes to this: What are you willing to defend? Use an honest assessment, and determine whether you feel justified in your selection and use. It is not necessarily a challenge when a parent questions your choices; sometimes it is just an opportunity for discus-sion. This can lead to enlightenment for both parties involved.

In this process, I urge you to use common sense (which, incidentally, is not so common). Common sense is your ability to be aware of and adapt to other people's needs. It is the "sense" gained from the knowledge of both specific subject matter and community. There is no magical technique to acquire it, no procedure to follow nor skills to be taught. I believe it can be developed only through practice and time. So, dive in, make mistakes, and learn from them.

References

Herald, D. *Genreflecting: A Guide to Reading Interests in Genre Fiction*. (3rd ed.). Englewood: Libraries Unlimited, 1995.

Karolides, N. J., L. Burress, & J. M. Kean, eds. *Censored Books: Critical Viewpoints*. Metuchen: Scarecrow Press, 1993.

Kies, C. *Presenting Young Adult Horror Fiction*. New York: Twayne Publishers, 1992.

PART 2

Lesson Plans and Programs

Mini Lessons:
Ideas and Activities

Sometimes you don't have the time or support to incorporate a full lesson. These activities can be used with any type of literature, but I've included some scary stories to use as examples.

Bio-Poems. Grades 3-6

These can be used after reading a folktale with a strong character, or in conjunction with writing epitaphs. Use the activity sheet in Figure 2.1 on an overhead transparency as a model for the class, and generate discussion by asking the following questions. In order to get to the poem, make a web or chart.

> Who is the main character?
> What is he or she like?
> Who else is important in the story?
> How does the main character feel about them?
> How do other characters feel about the main character?

The witches in these stories can be used as examples:

Cole, Joanna. *Bony-Legs*. Four Winds, 1983.
Oram, Hiawyn. *Baba Yaga & the Wise Doll*. Dutton, 1998.
Palatini, Margie. *Piggie Pie!* Clarion, 1995.

Make Fun Food. Any grade

Recipes abound for creepy treats. Here is one example, followed by other resources.

Ghosts in the Graveyard

Ingredients:

3 1/2 cups cold milk

2 packages of 4-serving instant chocolate pudding

1 tub non-dairy whipped topping, thawed

1 16-oz. package chocolate wafer cookies, crushed

Directions:

1. Make pudding as directed, with 3 1/2 cups milk. Let stand for five minutes.

2. Stir in three cups of whipped topping and half of the crushed cookies.

3. Spoon that combination into 13" x 9" pan.

4. Sprinkle with the remaining cookies.

5. Refrigerate one hour.

6. Decorate with candy corn, Milano cookies with writing "RIP" (graves), spoonfuls of whipped topping (ghosts), and gummy worms.

BIO-POEM ACTIVITY SHEET

1. First Name:_____

2. Four traits:_____

3. Related to:_____

4. Cares deeply for:_____

5. Who feels:_____

6. Who needs:_____

7. Who gives:_____

8. Who would like to see:_____

9. Living in or at:_____

Figure 2.1

Other Books:

Bauer, Caroline Feller. *Halloween: Stories and Poems* (Recipes included). J. B. Lippincott, 1989.

Dahl, Roald. *Roald Dahl's Revolting Recipes.* Viking, 1994.

Web Site with Recipes:

The Perpetual Preschool

<www.perpetualpreschool.com/halloweenart. html>

This site has great, quick activities that can be used at any grade level. The Halloween recipe section includes plenty of treats.

Critical Thinking: Details and Recollection. Any grade

Encourage students to practice observation skills, recall details, and distinguish false data. Read a book or story that can be completed in one sitting, and then ask questions to test recollection.

Example: *Lucy Dove* by Janice Del Negro. After losing her job as the laird's seamstress, Lucy sets her heart on reward money offered for stitching trousers by the light of the moon. There is one catch: She must stitch them in St. Andrew's graveyard, rumored to be haunted by a fearsome bogle.

    1. What is a laird?

    2. What are trews?

    3. What is a bogle?

    4. What is the first picture in the book? Why?

    5. What is the last picture of the book? Why?

    6. The chant of the bogle is "I want me skin and bones!" (True or False?)

Ask the students to work in groups to create their own questions and statements to share with the class.

Make a Tootsie Pop® Ghost. Grades K-2

This is a simple craft activity that can be combined with any ghost story.

Materials: Tootsie Pops, tissues or white cloth, markers and string
Directions: Tie the "sheet" over the "head" of the ghost. Use markers to add eyes and a mouth.

If you can find the book *The Ghost & I: Scary Stories for Participatory Telling* (Jennifer Justice), it contains an adaptation of the classic, *Going on a Bear Hunt* called "The Ghost Hunt." If you cannot find this book, simply substitute a ghost for the bear and walk through some creepy, cumbersome settings, such as a swamp, the woods, or a graveyard. When you find the ghost, turn around and run back FAST to your house and bed.

Sing Songs. Any grade

You can use songs and melodies included in some story collections, or you can take frightening poems, such as those included in Jack Prelutsky's *Nightmares: Poems to Trouble Your Sleep*, and sing them with a familiar melody.

Here is an example, with resources listed for other choices.

Old Woman All Skin and Bone
(Traditional folk song of America and Great Britain)

There was an old woman all skin and bone
Who lived near the graveyard all alone.
O-o-o-o-o-o!
She thought she'd go to church one day
To hear the parson preach and pray.
O-o-o-o-o-o!
And when she came to the church-house stile
She thought she'd stop and rest awhile.
O-o-o-o-o-o!
When she came up to the door
She thought she'd stop and rest some more.
O-o-o-o-o-o!

But when she turned and looked around
She saw a corpse upon the ground.
O-o-o-o-o-o!
From its nose down to its chin
The worms crawled out, and the worms crawled in.
O-o-o-o-o-o!
The woman to the preacher said,
"Shall I look like that when I am dead?"
O-o-o-o-o-o!
The preacher to the woman said,
"You'll look like that when you are dead!"
(Now scream:)
"AAAAAAAAAAAAH!"

Other books:

Goode, Diane. *Diane Goode's Book of Scary Stories & Songs.* Dutton, 1994.
Prelutsky, Jack. *Nightmares: Poems to Trouble Your Sleep.* Greenwillow, 1976.
Prelutsky, Jack. *The Headless Horseman Rides Tonight.* Mulberry, 1992.

Web site with Songs:

The Perpetual Preschool

<www.perpetualpreschool.com/halloween songs.html>
On this diverse site, go to the Halloween sections, and click on songs.

Retell a Story. Any grade, depending on story

No other genre sparks creative responses like horror. Ask students to tell a scary story, and they do so with ease. Students line up at the end of the school year to participate in this activity. Some share their own horrors; others take simple stories from the Alvin Schwartz books. Here is an example of a selection for fourth graders.

"The Velvet Ribbon"
There once was a woman who always wore a velvet ribbon around her neck. She was very beautiful, and a man fell deeply in love with her. He would ask her why she always wore this ribbon, but her response would be vague. He married her, and when he asked about the ribbon, his wife said, "When we grow older, and before I die, I will tell you why I wear it." The years passed, and sure enough, the woman grew ill. She pulled her husband close and whispered, "Now you will know why I always wear this ribbon. Please remove it from my neck." He took off the ribbon, and her head rolled onto the floor.

Keep the story very straight and bare bones, and allow the children to elaborate upon it. My favorite retelling included a dog, whose collar acted as the ribbon.

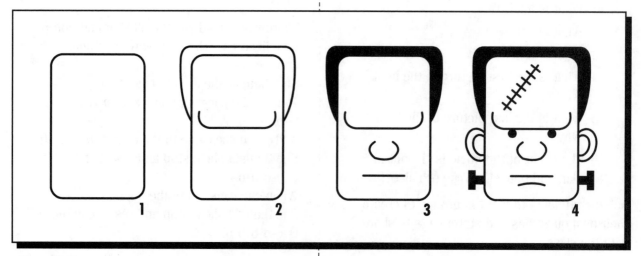

Figure 2.2

WORDS	GESTURES
Hi,	One palm up, as though gesturing "I don't know."
Ho,	Add second hand, same gesture.
For Halloween	Make a "mask" by forming a diamond with both index fingers touching and both middle fingers touching. Hold the mask in front of your eyes, then separate your hands, simultaneously bringing the index and middle fingers of each hand together.
When the Witches	Outline the triangle of a "witch hat" by touching together the tips of all fingers above your head and then separating your hands, bringing them down in a slanting movement.
all are seen,	Sign "see" by extending the index and middle fingers of each hand, then holding them in front of your eyes-as if your finger tips could see. Direct your fingers as though they are looking up at flying witches.
I wonder what this all could mean,	Gesture "I don't know" by holding both palms up at your sides and shrugging your shoulders. Let your face look puzzled. For musicality, bounce your arms slightly four times to the beat.
Hi, ho for Halloween.	Repeat the gestures for these words, above.

Figure 2.3

Use a Flannel board. Grades K-1

Some stories lend themselves to flannel board telling, and one of the easiest is "The Strange Visitor." It is found in numerous collections. As the body parts roll in, so do the felt pieces until the stranger is complete.

See:

Cecil, Laura. *Boo! Stories to Make You Jump.*
    Greenwillow, 1991
MacDonald, Margaret Read. *When the Lights Go Out: Twenty Scary Tales to Tell.*
    H. W. Wilson, 1988.

Draw Something Scary. Grades K-3

The Scary Book by Joanna Cole and Stephanie Calmenson contains step-by-step instructions by Chris Demarest on how to draw a monster, a werewolf, a witch, and a vampire. Illustrator's example shown in Figure 2.2.

Teach a Finger Play. Grades K-1

Storyteller Doug Lipman has included this one in *The Ghost & I: Scary Stories for Participatory Telling* (edited by Jennifer Justice).
See Figure 2.3.

Hi, Ho, for Halloween

Hi, ho, for Halloween,
When the <u>witches</u> all are seen,
I wonder what this all could mean,
Hi, ho, for Halloween!

"Hi, Ho, for Halloween" from *The Ghost & I: Scary Stories for Participatory Telling*. Edited by Jennifer Justice. Copyright © 1992 Yellow Moon Press. Reprinted by permission of Doug Lipman. <www.storydynamics.com>

Substitute other things for witches, such as ghosts, monsters, goblins, and vampires. Ask students to make new hand signs. Some examples might include fangs for the vampire and claws for the monsters.

Here's another example: **The Stirring Song.**

I'm stirring and stirring and stirring my brew. (Hold your hands together and pretend you're stirring something in a big pot.)

WHOO-OO, WHOO-OO (put hands near mouth and wiggle fingers).

I'm Stirring and stirring and stirring my brew (same hand action as before).

WHOO-OO, WHOO-OO (same finger action as before).

Tip-toe, tip-toe, tip-toe—BOO! (With each "tip-toe," sing lower and use your fingers to tip-toe in the air. When you get to "BOO," close and then open your hands next to your face, saying "BOO" loudly!)

This song, which was used at my daughter's preschool, is courtesy of Sue Jones; however, a printed version appears on **The Perpetual Preschool** Web site at <www.perpetual-preschool.com/halloweensongs.html> You can find many other songs and crafts on these pages.

Create a Story Pyramid. Grades 4-6

After listening to or reading a story, students fill in a pyramid, using the worksheet in Figure 2.4 as a guide. To complete it, they must fill in each line with the following information.

1. Name of the main character.
2. Two words describing the main character.
3. Three words describing the setting.
4. Four words stating the story problem.
5. Five words describing one event in the story.
6. Six words describing a second event.
7. Seven words describing a third event.
8. Eight words describing the solution to the problem.

Books to Use:

McKissack, Patricia. *The Dark-Thirty: Southern Tales of the Supernatural*. Knopf, 1992.

San Souci, Robert. *Even More Short and Shivery: Thirty Spine-Tingling Tales*. Delacorte Press, 1997.

Vivelo, Jackie. *Chills Run Down My Spine*. DK Ink, 1995.

STORY PYRAMID

1. ____
2. ____ ____
3. ____ ____ ____
4. ____ ____ ____ ____
5. ____ ____ ____ ____ ____
6. ____ ____ ____ ____ ____ ____
7. ____ ____ ____ ____ ____ ____ ____

Figure 2.4

Figure 2.5

Send an E-card for Halloween.
Grades 2-5

Resource:

E-Cards: Halloween

<www.e-cards.com/group/halloween/>
This is a fun, safe site for children, which contains cards, pumpkin contests, an interactive story, and Halloween history.

Things to try:
1. Send a card to each other or to a parent.
2. Model the interactive story. Each person adds a bit, and then sends the story as mail.

Easy Craft Projects. Any grade

After reading scary books, make a bookmark, bookplate, book bag, placemat, or calendar with scary decorations.

Materials: To decorate the item, use pictures from discarded books, original art, book jackets, posters featuring books, book catalogs, stencils, stickers, and other notions. You may want to laminate the item or cover it with contact paper.

More craft activities can be found in the magazine publication *Pack-o-Fun*. It is issued six times each year, and the October issue is full of Halloween crafts. Subscription information is available online at <www.craftideas.com> or by mail at:

> Pack-o-Fun
> PO Box 420235
> Palm Coast, FL 32142-0235

Have a Pumpkin Decorating Exhibit.
Any grade

This is a favorite every year in the library where I've worked. Students decorate (not carve) a pumpkin to look like their favorite scary character. It can be a literary character, an original monster, or one of the standard favorites (ghosts, witches, or vampires). Display all the pumpkins in the media center, and give each participant a small prize. It should be an exhibit, not a contest. See Figure 2.5.

Create a Newsletter. Grades 2-6

Using a desktop publisher, students create *The Deadly News*. The contents include summaries and humorous spin-offs of scary books, fake obituaries, epitaphs, and, in October, tips for Halloween safety. At the upper levels, students create their own advertisements to recruit gravediggers, promote new inventions, and encourage dead people to settle in a specific graveyard or haunted place. We also encourage personal ads, mock "interviews," and eyewitness reports.

Make a Paper Plate Mask. Grades K-1

Witches, monsters, and ghosts are easy to make. Children can add pipe cleaners, yarn, string, and other notions to create personal effects.

Make a Game Board with a Scary Theme. Any grade

There is a book called *Summer Reading Program Fun: 10 Thrilling, Inspiring, Wacky Board Games for Kids* by Wayne Johnson (ALA, 1999) that has two appropriate board games, "The Haunted Mansion" and "The Monster Bash." You can use the games that go with these boards, or create your own.

Invite a Guest. Any grade

As the librarian, you can schedule a local storyteller, guest speaker, parent, community worker or friend. A fresh face is always welcome.

One of the best experiences I've had working in the library was when the WILD THING arrived. Many costumes of literary characters are available for library use; best of all, they are almost free. You pay only for the shipping to the next location. Call early to reserve, and coordinate your efforts with neighboring libraries. The best resource is:

Costume Specialists
211 North Fifth Street
Columbus, Ohio 43215
Phone (800) 596-9357 fax (614) 464-2114

Or visit the Library PR Web site at <www.ssde sign.com/librarypr/content/p121697a.shtml> for complete details.

Make A Witch Brew. Any Grade

In Margaret Read McDonald's book, *When the Lights Go Out: Twenty Scary Tales to Tell,* there is a great "recipe" for a brew. If you can't find this book, simply buy an assortment of plastic webs, rats, frogs, and eyes, and mix them in a cauldron with colored slimy water. Add a splash of bromo seltzer, and watch the brew fizz.

Book:

MacDonald, Margaret Read. *When the Lights Go Out: Scary Stories to Tell.* H. W. Wilson, 1988.

Lessons:
English Language Arts

Create a Monster Book. Grades K-1

Objectives:

Students will:

1. Develop a familiarity with stories dealing with fear and monsters.
2. Discuss what makes a monster "scary."
3. Use their imaginations to create a monster.
4. Use humor to put a monster in a household setting.
5. Draw their monster in the setting.
6. Use letter recognition and sounds to name their monster.
7. Compile a book with all of the monsters.

Resources:

Picture Books:

Emberley, Ed. *Go Away, Big Green Monster!* Little, Brown, 1993.

Hoban, Russell. *Monsters*. Scholastic, 1989.

Leuck, Laura. *My Monster Mama Loves Me So*. Lothrop, Lee & Shepard, 1999.

Mayer, Mercer. *There's a Nightmare in My Closet*. Dial, 1968.

Namm, Diane. *Monsters!* Children's Press, 1990.

O'Keefe, Susan. *One Hungry Monster: A Counting Book in Rhyme*. Joy Street/Little, Brown, 1989.

Rosenberg, Liz. *Monster Mama*. Philomel, 1993.

Materials:

Paper, pencils, art supplies, bookmaking materials (binder, laminator)

Procedure:

1. Teacher and students discuss fears: of nighttime, of monsters, of dying, or whatever else emerges.
2. Teacher reads a variety of stories from list and encourages feedback.
3. Since many of the stories show how to deal with fear in a humorous way, teacher may prompt discussion in this manner.
4. Teacher explains that students can now create their own monster. It can look like any monster they imagine; it does not have to be one they have seen. It can even be a combination of two monsters. The monster may be drawn in whatever style the child can create.
5. Teacher will ask students to think of a silly spot where the monster could be in their house—perhaps in a younger sibling's high chair, the bathtub, or the laundry basket?

What face would that monster be making? Why? Would it still be scary?

6. After students have thought this through, they will draw a monster in their house.
7. Students will name the monster.
8. Teacher compiles the monsters and assembles a book to be shared.

Descriptive Words for Witches.
Grades K-4

Objectives:

Students will:

1. Explore books that have a witch in the story.
2. Compare and contrast "good" and "bad" witches.
3. Determine through written clues adjectives to describe witches.
4. Determine through visual clues action verbs to describe witches.
5. Generate a list of descriptive words for good and bad witches.
6. Create a picture of a witch and add appropriate descriptive words.

Resources:

Wicked Witches:

Carlson, Natalie Savage. *Spooky and the Witch's Goat*. Lothrop, Lee & Shepard, 1989.

Hearn, Diane Dawson. *Bad Luck Boswell*. Simon & Schuster, 1995.

Johnson, Paul Brett. *A Perfect Pork Stew*. Orchard, 1998.

Steig, William. *Wizzil*. Farrar, 2000.

Wood, Audrey. *Heckedy Peg*. Harcourt, 1987.

(You can also include any of the Baba Yaga books as portraits of wicked witches.)

Good Witches:

Glassman, Peter. *My Working Mom*. Morrow, 1994.

Kellogg, Steven. *The Christmas Witch*. Dial, 1992.

Lodge, Bernard. *Mouldylocks*. Houghton Mifflin, 1998.

Rosner, Ruth. *Nattie Witch*. Harper & Row, 1989.

Stevenson, James. *Emma*. Greenwillow, 1985.

Procedure:

1. Teacher reads two selections, contrasting the portrayal of the witch.
2. Students and teacher discuss instances where witches have been portrayed as wicked or kind (for example, in *The Wizard of Oz*). Through discussion, a list of descriptive words can be generated. Concepts to consider include:

    What kind of clothing does the witch wear?

    What color skin and hair does she have?

    What facial features are described?

    Where does the witch live?

    With whom does she live?

    What does she eat?

    What kind of spells does she create?

    How does she travel?

3. Using the actual text and illustrations, list descriptive phrases (adjectives) and actions (verbs) that may not have been included in discussion. Have students fill in the chart in Figure 2.6. To clarify actions with younger students, you may want to modify the chart to read:

    GOOD WITCHES DO:
    GOOD WITCHES DON'T:

    BAD WITCHES DO:
    BAD WITCHES DON'T

4. Students fold a piece of paper in half and create a picture of a witch using a variety of media. They do not label the witch in any way.
5. After collecting the pictures, teacher redistributes them, asking students to use adjectives and verbs to describe the witch.

CHART - WORDS TO DESCRIBE WITCHES

STORY 1: (GOOD WITCH) TITLE	STORY 2: (BAD WITCH) TITLE
Describe the witch's:	Describe the witch's:
Clothing	Clothing
Hair	Hair
Face	Face
Features	Features
Home	Home
Family members	Family members
Diet (Food)	Diet (Food)
Spells (Magic)	Spells (Magic)
Travel	Travel
What does the witch do? (Actions)	What does the witch do? (Actions)
GOOD WITCHES DO:	BAD WITCHES DO:
GOOD WITCHES DON'T:	BAD WITCHES DON'T:

Figure 2.6

Comparing Folktales. Grades 3-6

Objectives:

Students will:

1. Listen to two versions of the same folktale and discuss similarities and differences.
2. Use the think, pair, and share strategy to share their ideas with classmates in an organized style.
3. Read stories to compare and contrast.
4. Organize a folktale for retelling.
5. Present a folktale in an oral setting.

Resources:

Find these folktales in picture books or story collections.

"Wiley and the Hairy Man." Wiley and his mom must trick the conjuring Hairy Man three times before he will leave them alone.

> Bang, Molly. *Wiley and the Hairy Man.* Macmillan, 1976.
> Low, Alice. *Spooky Stories for a Dark & Stormy Night.* Hyperion, 1994.
> Pepper, Dennis, ed. *The Oxford Book of Scary Tales.* Oxford University Press, 1992.
> Sierra, Judy. *Wiley and the Hairy Man.* Dutton, 1996.

"Wait 'Till Martin Comes." A man is terrified at the thought of meeting the leader of wild cats.

> Cole, Joanna, and Stephanie Calmenson. *The Scary Book.* Morrow Junior Books, 1991.
> Leach, Maria. *The Thing at the Foot of the Bed and Other Scary Tales.* Putnam, 1987.
> Schwartz, Alvin. *Scary Stories to Tell in the Dark.* HarperCollins, 1986.

"Taily-Po." After someone chops off an animal's tail, the animal comes back to claim its parts.

> Cole, Joanna, and Stephanie Calmenson. *The Scary Book.* Morrow Junior Books, 1991.

> Galdone, Joanna. *The Tailypo: A Ghost Story.* Clarion, 1984.
> Smith, Jimmy Neil, ed. *Homespun: Tales from America's Favorite Storytellers.* Crown, 1988.

"The Viper." He's coming up the stairs, and he "vants to vipe your vindows."

> Cole, Joanna, and Stephanie Calmenson. *The Scary Book.* Morrow Junior Books, 1991.
> O'Malley, Kevin. *Velcome.* Walker, 1997.
> Schwartz, Alvin. *Scary Stories to Tell in the Dark.* HarperCollins, 1986.

"The Tinker and the Ghost." Someone is rewarded for staying the night at a haunted house or graveyard.

> Del Negro, Janice. *Lucy Dove.* DK Ink., 1998.
> Galdone, Paul. *The Monster and the Tailor.* Clarion, 1982.
> Hancock, Sibyl. *Esteban and the Ghost.* Dial, 1983.

Procedure:

1. Read two versions of any of the common folk tales listed, or choose one of your own.
2. Discuss with students the concept of think, pair, and share. Students do exactly that, with a partner, and share with the class appropriately as directed by the teacher.
3. Ask students questions about how the tales were alike and different in the areas of:

> Setting
>
> Characters
>
> Length
>
> Ending
>
> Illustrations (if appropriate)
>
> Moral (if applicable)

Also ask if the students know of any other story similar to the one read.

Students answer in the think, pair, and share format.

4. Share in a retelling of the story, modeling a graphic organizer to help. The organizer can be a storyboard, story web, outline, chart (as shown in Figure 2.8), or other design. Students can add their "voices" to the retelling, emphasizing certain words, descriptions, or other aspects they enjoyed.

5. Have student pairs read two versions of a story. You may need to read the story to them, depending on their ability.

6. As a pair, they must fill in the chart shown in Figure 2.7.

7. As a pair, they must decide how to retell the story. They can combine the best elements of both stories, use one as the sole resource, or incorporate their own ideas to mix into the general plot. They should use a graphic organizer as modeled in the lesson.

8. Working together, the students retell the story in an oral setting.

Writing an Epitaph. Grades 3-6

Objectives:

Students will:

1. Listen to epitaphs written by professionals and other writers.

2. Learn the two-line structure (aa) and rhyme scheme to make a short epitaph.

3. Create an epitaph based on either the poetic form described above or an elaboration.

Resources:

Story:

Goode, Diane. "Tain't So!" *Diane Goode's Book of Scary Stories and Songs.* Dutton, 1994.

Epitaphs: either from tombstones or use:

Bauer, Caroline Feller. *Halloween: Stories and Poems.* J. B. Lippincott, 1989.

Materials:

Rhyming dictionary, pencil, scissors, paper

Procedure:

1. Students listen to epitaphs.

2. Teacher introduces poetic form of the two-line (aa) rhyme scheme.

3. Teacher encourages students to create a silly epitaph, one that would describe a death that would never happen in real life.

4. Teacher teaches skills to use rhyming dictionary.

5. Teacher writes one epitaph with students as practice.

6. Students write an epitaph. It can be in the "aa" style, or an elaboration thereof.

7. Students print epitaphs on white paper cut to resemble a tombstone.

8. Teacher can enhance activity with stories about those who need to read their epitaph in order to be convinced of their death.

Examples: (from Caroline Feller Bauer's book *Halloween: Stories and Poems*)

1. Here lies the body of our Anna
   Done to death by a banana.

2. It was a cough that carried her off.
   It was a coffin they carried her off in.

See also:

Education World (lesson plans)

<www.education-
    world.com/a_curr/curr033.shtml>
Education World is a teacher resource full of lesson plans. This lesson plan is similar to the epitaph lesson listed above, and provides more examples.

COMPARE FOLKTALES

NAME_____

STORY 1: (TITLE)	STORY 2: (TITLE)
List the characters here:	List the characters here:
Where did the story take place? (Setting)	Where did the story take place? (Setting)

What happened during the story's:
  Beginning:
	What happened during the story's:
	  Beginning:

Middle:	Middle:
End:	End:
Comment on the illustrations, if any:	Comment on the illustrations, if any:
Best part of story:	Best part of story:
Who is the author?	Who is the author?
Are there illustrations? Do they enhance the story?	Are there illustrations? Do they enhance the story?

Figure 2.7

CHART ORGANIZER

Characters:

Actions:

Setting:

Beginning:

Middle:

End:

Figure 2.8

Lessons: Social Studies

Architecture Throughout History.

Grades 5-6

Objectives:

Students will:

1. Understand the architecture of various time periods.

2. Determine how architecture was reflective of culture and changes.

3. Compare and contrast architectural forms in Europe and North America.

4. Listen to works of supernatural phenomena and recognize characteristics of the "haunted house."

Resources:

Haunted House Stories, Locations and History:

Bunting, Eve. *Night of the Gargoyles.* Clarion, 1994.

Cohen, Daniel. *Ghost in the House.* Cobblehill, 1993.

Kettelkamp, Larry. *Haunted Houses.* Morrow, 1969.

Vivelo, Jackie. "Chills Run Down My Spine." *Chills Run Down My Spine.* DK Ink, 1995.

Wood, Ted. *Ghosts of the Southwest: The Phantom Gunslinger and Other Real-Life Hauntings.* Walker, 1997.

Wood, Ted. *Ghosts of the West Coast: The Lost Souls of the Queen Mary and Other Real-Life Hauntings.* Walker, 1999.

Architectural References: These resources can give structural resources and facts.

Chrisp, Peter. *The Colosseum.* Raintree Steck-Vaughn, 1997.

> A 48-page illustrated book that describes the planning and building of the Colosseum in ancient Rome and tells how it was used.

Chrisp, Peter. *The Middle Ages.* Two-Can (F. Watts), 1997.

> An illustrated 32-page book that includes information about homes, castles, markets, tournaments, and beliefs of the people of the time.

Chrisp, Peter. *The Parthenon.* Raintree Steck-Vaughn, 1997.

> The planning, building, and uses of the Parthenon in 48 illustrated pages.

Janson, H. W., and Anthony Janson. *History of Art for Young People.* Harry Abrams, 1997.

> A 632-page volume that includes architectural reference from the earliest known time to the present.

Parker, Steve. *What's Inside Buildings?* Peter Bedrick Books, 1995.

> A general, introductory 44-page book

that covers basic structural aspects and highlights special features of specific buildings.

Internet Resources for Architectural Reference:

Architecture Through the Ages

<tqjunior.advanced.org/3786/index.html# Ancient>
This site is an age-appropriate study of major movements in architectural history. Written by students, it gives pictures and concise summaries of the features relevant to each period.

Medieval Culture as Evidenced by Gargoyles

<web.lemoyne.edu/museums/begieral/muse um.html>
This site strives to show the relationship between gargoyles and the ideology, religion and architecture of the time period. It includes a section just for kids.

Procedure:

1. Students and teacher discuss and share characteristics of the haunted house as under stood and experienced today.

2. Teacher explains some basic foundations of architecture and introduces the concept that art and architecture of a society are influenced by religion, politics, population, and cultural ideas.

3. Students share any examples they may know; for example, structural forms and art works discussing the possible influences reflected in the work.

4. Teacher assigns one of five eras—Byzantine, Baroque, Romanesque/Gothic, Modern, or Renaissance—to a group of students to research.

5. Using research materials, students answer questions relating to their time period.

   Examples include but are not limited to:

   a) What is the meaning of "_____" (a listed time period)?

b) What was happening in Europe at the height of the period?

c) What major European countries were dominant during this period?

d) What was the characteristic of European culture at this time? (For example, was it a time of exploration, colonization, wealth, or poverty?)

e) How did (time period) architecture influence North American architecture?

6. Students obtain, draw, or create (using computer graphics or other method) an example of their time period's architecture. The example should be labeled with important characteristics of that style, such as flying buttress or columns.

7. Teacher constructs a time line, and as students complete research, each group gives a short oral report on time period and architecture, placing graphic in correct position on the time line.

8. Teacher and students discuss which form of architecture has been most influential on today's haunted house and why.

9. Teacher discusses the term "phenomenon," both supernatural and physical, and shares examples. Sharing can include excerpts from any nonfiction source or story sharing from collections above.

10. Students write a story combining elements of history, architecture, culture, and phenomenon.

Historical Ghosts of Battles and Wars.
Grades 4-6

Objectives:

Students will:

1. Plan, write, and edit an original personified historical account.

2. Listen to and read ghost stories of noted individuals or historical eras.

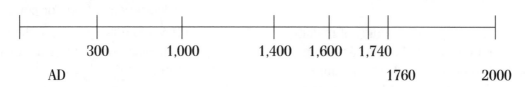

NAME_____

TIME LINE

```
|-------|-------|-------|---|--||-------------|
       300     1,000   1,400 1,600 1,740
                                            1,760        2,000
   AD
```

1. Place each time period in the correct spot on the time line.
   Byzantine, Baroque, Romanesque/Gothic, Modern, Renaissance

2. List two periods where religious powers were most dominant. What can you say about the duration (length of time) of these periods?

   _____

   _____

   _____

3. Short essay:

   1. Describe two features of Gothic architecture that you feel are artistic, and then relate those features to a modern "haunted house."

   or

   2. Based upon your knowledge of architecture and supernatural phenomena, write a story involving a haunted house. Include the time period in which it was built, and provide details about the structure of the house. Include at least one supernatural phenomenon.

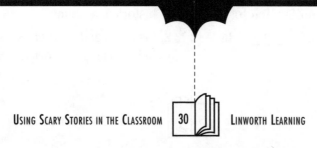

Figure 2.9

3. Research a historical period that relates to a noted ghost story.

4. Write a short paper that incorporates the historical era and the situation resulting in the ghostly appearance.

Resources:

Ghost Stories:

Cohen, Daniel. *Civil War Ghosts*. Scholastic, 1999.

Cohen, Daniel. *Ghost in the House*. Cobblehill, 1993.

Cohen, Daniel. *Ghostly Tales of Love and Revenge*. Putnam, 1992.

Cohen, Daniel. *Great Ghosts*. Dutton, 1990.

Cohen, Daniel. *The Ghosts of War*. Putnam, 1990.

Grinnel, George Bird, comp., and John Bierhorst, ed. *The Whistling Skeleton: American Indian Tales of the Supernatural*. Scholastic, 1982.

Leach, Maria. *Whistle in the Graveyard*. ("Famous Ghosts" section). Viking, 1974.

Windham, Kathryn Tucker, and Margaret Gillis Figh. *13 Alabama Ghosts and Jeffrey*. Strode Publishers, 1969.

Windham, Kathryn Tucker, and Margaret Gillis Figh. *13 Georgia Ghosts and Jeffrey*. Strode Publishers, 1973.

> Although these books are out of print, if you can get them through inter-library loan, you will not be disappointed. They contain stories of the South that relate to specific locations, such as

Huntingdon College in Alabama and the Bonaventure estate in Georgia.

Historical Books Relating to Time Periods:

Many of the mentioned story collections have introductions with historical information. Additionally, you can use information you find in trade or textbooks.

Procedure:

1. Determine the historical era appropriate for the grade level you teach.

2. Have students listen to a historical ghost story. The story "Grief" from *Ghostly Tales of Love and Revenge* is a perfect example of a ghost tale woven into historical fact. It is the story of Marion Hooper Adams' monument in Washington D.C.

3. Allow students time to read and research their own ghost story, using collections listed above or other resources. The ghost must be a documented account of a real person, not a folktale of any generic restless spirit.

4. Additionally, students should generate background information pertaining to the events/lifestyle common in the living day of his or her chosen ghost. (See Figure 2.10.)

5. Students synthesize the historical information with the legend of the ghost and create a personified history story. They must use the first person when writing. (See Figure 2.10.)

6. Students share the stories with classmates.

GHOST STORY: BACKGROUND HISTORICAL INFORMATION

NAME_____

Your ghost's name: _____

The year(s) your ghost was alive: _____

Where did your ghost live? _____

Who lived with him or her? _____

Do you know what kind of:

1. Food was eaten by the ghost, the ghost's family, or other people?

_____

2. Clothes were worn by your ghost (fancy, shabby, animal hide, rags)?

_____

3. House or structure your ghost or ghost's family lived in? _____

_____

4. Weapons/tools/utensils were used at the time your ghost was alive? _____

_____

5. Customs for marriage were important when your ghost was alive? _____

_____

6. Conflict or war was happening that might have been important to your ghost?

_____

7. Money or wealth your ghost or your ghost's family had? How did they show their wealth? Or, how did you know people were rich in those days?

_____

_____

Was your ghost romantically involved (in love) with someone? _____
Who? _____
Was someone in love with your ghost? _____

Figure 2.10

HISTORICAL GHOST STORY PLANNING SHEET

NAME_____

You must write the story as if you are the ghost today. In your story, tell your audience how you lived, who lived with you, what was important to people at the time you were alive, and how you died. To help you plan the story, you can use a story web, storyboard, outline, or other graphic organizer. This is a checklist for the "ingredients" of your story.

What you need to include:	(Y/N) Included?
Your name (as the ghost)	_____
When you lived	_____
Who you lived with	_____
How old you were when you died	_____
How you died	_____
Details discovered in your research relating to:	
Family	_____
Food	_____
Wealth	_____
Love life	_____
What you actually do today to scare or bother people	_____
Why you still roam the earth	_____

Figure 2.11

Lessons: Science

The Human Skeleton. Grades 2-6

Objectives:

Students will:

1. Compare their preconceptions about the skeleton with a model of a human skeleton.

2. Research and examine a skeleton to accurately draw and label human bones.

3. Listen to and discuss folklore involving skeletal beings.

Resources:

Stories:

DeFelice, Cynthia. *The Dancing Skeleton*. Macmillan, 1989

Leach, Maria. "The Singing Bone." *The Thing at the Foot of the Bed and Other Scary Tales*. Putnam, 1987. (Also told in *The Magic Orange Tree* by Diane Wolkstein).

McDonald, Megan. *The Bone Keeper*. DK Ink, 1999.

Olson, Arielle, and Howard Schwartz. "The Hand of Death." *Ask the Bones: Scary Stories from Around the World*. Viking, 1999.

San Souci, Robert. "The Hundredth Skull" *A Terrifying Taste of Short & Shivery: Thirty Creepy Tales*. Delacorte Press, 1998.

Schwartz, Alvin. "Aaron Kelly's Bones." *Scary Stories to Tell in the Dark*. HarperCollins, 1986.

Schwartz, Alvin. "Old Woman All Skin and Bone." *Scary Stories to Tell in the Dark*. HarperCollins, 1986.

Schwartz, Alvin. "The Thing." *Scary Stories to Tell in the Dark*. HarperCollins, 1986.

Non-Fiction Books:

Hawcock, David. *The Amazing Pull-Out Pop-Up Body in a Book*. DK Publishing, 1997.
    A three-dimensional tour of the body, with moving flaps and levers.

Llewellyn, Claire. *The Big Book of Bones: An Introduction to Skeletons*. Peter Bedrick Books, 1998.
    48 pages of moving skeletal pictures and bone facts.

Simon, Seymour. *Bones: Our Skeletal System*. Morrow Junior Books, 1998.
    A picture book of the skeletal system, with x-ray photography and photos of bone structures.

Materials:

Paper (long rolls), markers, model of the human skeleton

Procedure:

1. Divide students into partners. Have each partner draw the other's body outline as the student lies on the paper.

2. Without referring to text, each student draws his or her skeleton in the outline.

3. Hang drawings while students gather information about the skeletal system.

4. As students gather information, they will record and map it on a second body outline, leaving space on the paper for drawing bones.

5. Students take turns constructing the model properly and then complete the second drawing of the skeleton in the second body outline.

6. Read stories.

7. Students respond creatively with a short story, mystery or poem.

(This lesson was adapted from the Sonoma State University Web site at <www.sonoma.edu/>.)

Mummification. Grade 6

Objectives:

Students will:

1. Experience the scientific process.

2. Develop process skills and document the process.

3. Develop an understanding that mummification was an essential part of the religion of Ancient Egypt.

4. Share and respond to stories related to project.

Resources:

Stories:

Bellairs, John. *The Mummy, the Will and the Crypt*. Dial, 1983.

Bunting, Eve. *I am the Mummy Heb-Nefert*. Harcourt Brace, 1997. (Picture book)

Byars, Betsy. *McMummy*. Viking, 1993.

Coffin, M. T. *Escape from the Haunted Museum*. Avon Books, 1996.

Greenberg, Martin. *Mummy Stories*. Severn House Publishers Ltd., 1991.

Hall, Katy. *Mummy Riddles*. Dial, 1997.

Karr, Kathleen. *Gideon and the Mummy Professor*. Farrar, 1993.

Voigt, Cynthia. *The Vandemark Mummy*. Atheneum, 1991.

Whitcher, Susan. "Hieroglyphics." *Real Mummies Don't Bleed: Friendly Tales for October Nights*. Farrar, 1993.

Woodruff, Elvira. *The Magnificent Mummy Maker*. Scholastic, 1994.

Non-Fiction Books for Research: You can use any of the mummy trade books that may be available, and you may want to look for these titles as well.

Deary, Terry, and Peter Hepplewhite. *The Awesome Egyptians*. Scholastic, 1993.
This book is part of the *Horrible Histories* series. The author makes Egyptians amazing to read about and fun for children's levels of humor.

Deem, James M. *How to Make a Mummy Talk*. Houghton Mifflin, 1995.
This resource includes 184 pages with drawings that share the historical importance of mummies, focusing more on history than on death.

Getz, David. *Frozen Girl*. Holt, 1998.
These 80 pages describe a 13-year-old Inca girl found frozen and mummified. Illustrations, scientific explanations and actual photos are included.

Stewart, David. *You Wouldn't Want to Be an Egyptian Mummy!: Disgusting Things You'd Rather Not Know*. Franklin Watts, 2001.
Exactly what the title admits, some of the facts regarding mummification are not pretty.

Web sites:

Corkankhamoun Explains Mummification

<members.aol.com/mumifyddog/index.html>

This is a fun site at which you can mail e-cards, play Egyptian MadLibs, try Mancala, and color in the coloring book.

Sea World Bush Gardens – Egypt Fun Guide

<www.seaworld.org/Egypt/egypt.html>

An age-appropriate educational resource that provides information and learning games. Topics include hieroglyphics, cartouches, pyramids, the Nile, and more.

Materials:

One whole chicken for each group of four to six students, plastic gloves, salt, spices, paper towels, gallon-size zippered freezer bags, gauze strips, plastic containers to hold chicken in the bag in case of leakage.

PLEASE NOTE * As a health precaution, this lesson will require gloves for all stages of meat handling. Please inform parents prior to starting the lesson.

Procedure:

1. Students will keep a journal of their process, findings, and responses.

2. Wearing gloves, students will remove entrails from chicken. These can either be discarded or saved in baby food jars. The jars then can be decorated with clay heads of Egyptian gods.

3. At a sink, rinse chicken inside and out until all liquid runs clear.

4. With a large supply of paper towels, dry the chicken inside and out. This is critical, as moisture creates problems in the process.

5. Using about 1/2 cup of any inexpensive fragrant spice, rub the spice all over the chicken. The spice will mask the odor of decay.

6. Each group uses one whole 26-ounce container of table salt. (Egyptians used natron; salt is the closest thing to this.) Rub salt over the entire chicken. The chicken must be absolutely dry, and every inch must be covered.

7. Fill the cavity with salt.

8. Place each chicken in the zippered freezer bag. Seal. Place in waterproof tubs, away from direct sunlight.

9. Once a week for four or five weeks, someone must open the bag and drain the liquid. Each chicken must be re-salted, re-spiced, and placed in a clean bag. Also refill the cavity with salt. During this time, there can be an immersion in Egyptian folklore and tales. It is a perfect time to introduce stories of famous mummies and of mummies stalking the earth.

10. Repeat this process until there is no more accumulation of liquid in the bags. Continue the immersion in literature. As students become more familiar with stories and their mummy, they will want to name the chicken and write a creative response to their experience.

11. Wrap the mummy in gauze strips or ripped muslin strips. Decorate with "authentic" Egyptian amulets, medallions, and jewels.

12. Students can create a sarcophagus and a history for their mummy. Use shoe boxes. Spray box with gravel paint. Decorate with hieroglyphics and pictures of Egyptian gods.

13. Students can bury the sarcophagus and dig it up in a few months. The mummy will be in the same condition.

14. Students will share their stories.

* Adapted from an AskERIC Lesson (AELP-SPS0012). Submitted by Connie Armstrong, Madison No. 1 Middle School, 5525 North 16th Street, Phoenix, AZ 85016, with special thanks to Mimi Norton, Solano Elementary.

Lesson: Math

Pumpkin Math. Grades 2-4

Objectives:

Students will:

1. Make predictions based on size.
2. Measure and weigh pumpkins, and record data in charts.
3. Compare data from various pumpkins.
4. Find relationships through observation.
5. Listen to stories to enhance appreciation.

Materials:

Pumpkins, scale, tape measure, chart paper, materials to hollow out a pumpkin

Resources:

Stories:

Johnston, Tony. *Very Scary*. Harcourt Brace, 1995.

Kroll, Steven. *The Biggest Pumpkin Ever*. Holiday House, 1984.

Martin, Bill, Jr. *The Magic Pumpkin*. H. Holt, 1989.

Silverman, Erica. *Big Pumpkin*. Simon & Schuster, 1992.

Stallings, Fran. "The Story of a Pumpkin." *The Ghost and I: Scary Stories for Participatory Telling*. Ed. Jennifer Justice. Yellow Moon Press, 1992.

White, Linda. *Too Many Pumpkins*. Holiday House, 1996.

Web sites:

World Class Giant Pumpkins

<www.backyardgardener.com/wcgp/index.html>

This site has recorded the weights of the biggest pumpkins in the world.

Plant Answers: PUMPKIN

<aggie-horticulture.tamu.edu/PLANTanswers/ vegetables/pumpkin.html>

Basic horticulture information is presented in a question-and-answer format.

Pumpkin Masters

<www.pumpkinmasters.com/contest.html>

This commercial site of pumpkin carving supplies includes a beautiful page of award-winning carved pumpkins.

Procedure:

1. Pick three pumpkins and predict their weights.
2. Record weight predictions.
3. Weigh pumpkins.
4. Organize predictions and actual weights on a chart.
5. Measure the circumference of the pumpkins and record.
6. Discuss the relationship between the weight and circumference. Does the heaviest pumpkin have the largest circumference?
7. Predict which pumpkin will have the most seeds. Record predictions.
8. Hollow out pumpkins and count seeds.
9. Read stories to promote further enjoyment of the pumpkin activities.

Lesson: Technology

Comparing Scary Stories in a World Classroom. Grades: 5-6

Objectives:

Students will:

1. Share information about their town and their culture.
2. Respond to and analyze the writing of other authors.
3. Learn about the culture and customs of life in other places.
4. Examine beliefs in relation to others.
5. Use technology and the Internet to communicate, cooperate, and correspond with students in other places.

Resources:

A safe resource to connect students to other classrooms can be found at:

ePALS Classroom Exchange

With Scholastic as a supporter, ePALS now claims to be the largest online classroom community. In addition to connecting to other classrooms, you can use free e-mail, lesson plans, chat rooms, and educational products.

Procedure:

This can be done in conjunction with a unit on folklore, which can then be enhanced with local scary lore. It also can be an exercise in creative writing, drawing strictly upon the students' imagination and placed in a local setting.

1. Students describe the first local, creepy place they would take a foreign visitor and tell what makes that place scary. They are to use details and incorporate feelings.
2. Students describe an incident that may or may not have happened in that place. The story can be local legend or an original creation by the student.
3. Each student submits one piece of written work, composed offline. A print version will remain with the teacher.
4. Writing is then submitted online.
5. Written exchanges from students in other parts of the country and world are printed, read, and discussed in class. The submissions are read in small groups of four, and then reported to the class. The more submissions that are read, the more critical the students will become.
6. Students submit one response to these readings (composed offline).
7. At the end of the unit, each small group will create a presentation about what was learned from the exchange with students in other places. Presentation may be oral, written, visual, or a combination of all three.

Lesson: Art

Artistic Styles of Tombstones.

Grades 5-6

I actually remember doing this lesson in my junior high art class. It was morbid then, and it still is!

Objectives:

Students will:

1. Research styles of tombstones and graves found in local cemetery.
2. Use scrollwork, calligraphy, and tracings to create a reproduction of a tomb.
3. Listen and respond to spooky and humorous stories of graveyards and the dead.
3. Compose a postcard incorporating the words and style of a tomb.

Resources:

Stories:

Coville, Bruce. "The Secret of City Cemetery." *Bruce Coville's Book of Ghosts: Tales to Haunt You*. Scholastic, 1994.

Leach, Maria. "'Tain't So." *Whistle in the Graveyard*. Viking, 1974. (Retold in other collections, including *Diane Goode's Book of Scary Stories & Songs* and as "Dinkins is Dead" in Robert San Souci's *A Terrifying Taste of Short and Shivery*. Delacorte, 1998.)

Pepper, Dennis, ed. "Dare You." *The Oxford Book of Scarytales*. Oxford University Press, 1992. (Retold in other folktale collections, as "The Dare" in Maria Leach's *The Thing at the Foot of the Bed* and as "The Girl Who Stood on a Grave" in *Scary Stories to Tell in the Dark*.)

Pepper, Dennis, ed. "My Great-Grandfather's Grave Digging." *The Oxford Book of Scary Tales*. Oxford University Press, 1992.

Web site:

Find a Grave Site

This site has photographs and locations of thousands of grave markers. You can search by name, date of birth or death, and location.

Materials:

Butcher paper, crayons, calligraphy pens, scrolling paper, postcard templates (Figure 2.12), and oak tag

Procedure:

1. Students take a trip to local cemetery. They read the graves and have a discussion concerning who died, what the tombs look like, how old the stones are, and other factors,

both historical and artistic. If this cannot be arranged, visit the *Find a Grave* Web site, which contains thousands of photos.

2. Students trace (or copy from the Internet) their favorite grave by rubbing crayon over paper placed on the tomb. This is then brought back to the school.

3. Teacher instructs students on how to use their tombstone information to create a post card. The front of the card will be a pictorial representation of the tomb. The back will be a postcard from the dead.

4. The teacher demonstrates styles of calligraphy and instructs students on writing techniques.

5. Teacher demonstrates scroll work (rolled paper) to be used as ornamentation to post card.

6. While students work on project, teacher reads some spooky stories involving grave yards and the dead.

7. Students create a short letter from the dead based upon their interpretation of the experience and the stories.

BLANK POST CARD

To:

_____

_____

Figure 2.12

Annotations

In this section, you will find citations grouped by format. Included are picture books, I-Can-Read easy chapter books, transitional fiction for younger readers, novels, story collections, poetry and riddles, series, audiovisual materials, Web sites, and professional resources. Each annotation contains bibliographic information, a short summary with highlights, and review information, if available. I have limited the list to titles published within the last 15 years, making some exceptions for older materials that remain popular. Examples include *Where the Wild Things Are* (Sendak, 1963), *The Witches* (Dahl, 1983), and *Nightmares: Poems to Trouble Your Sleep* (Prelutsky, 1976). This does not mean that all titles listed are in print; on the contrary, many titles run one printing and then disappear, like the ghostly apparitions so common in their plots. The titles included should be available in most large public libraries if they are not found within your collection.

The 🔊 icon indicates a book that can be found in audio format, and the 🎥 icon signifies a video. Full bibliographic information is listed in the audiovisual section.

A note about reviews: I have tried to include at least two sources for each title, primarily using *Booklist* as it would designate a favorable review. Many of the materials have received excellent reviews, but you should judge a work for yourself and use the reviews simply to sup-

port your choices. I have included the following sources:

BL: Booklist

Book Links

BR: The Book Report

CCB-B: Center for Children's Book Bulletin

CM: Reviewing Journal of Canadian Material for Young People

CBRS: Children's Book Review Service

CBW: Children's Book Watch

EL: Emergency Librarian

GP: Growing Point: Review Guide for British Works

HB: Horn Book

HBG: Horn Book Guide

JB: Junior Bookshelf

Kliatt: Kliatt Young Adult Paperback Guide

KR: Kurkus Review

LA: Language Arts

LT: Library Talk

NYTBR: New York Times Book Review

PW: Publishers Weekly

RT: Reading Teacher

SL: School Librarian

SLJ: School Library Journal

VOYA: Voice of Youth Advocates

Picture Books:

When using picture books, stories for the youngest audiences typically are not scary. These books introduce the characters of the supernatural and Halloween, often teaching children how to cope with fear. More sophisticated picture books can be quite frightening and extremely entertaining when presented to older audiences.

Ackerman, Karen. *The Banshee*. Philomel, 1990. Illustrator: David Ray. Grades K-2
> The wailing banshee, a traditional figure of the supernatural, is subdued in this dark picture book with sparse text. As night falls, the banshee appears at a cozy village, attempting to find a lost soul to accompany her back into darkness. As she repeatedly fails, light comes, and with it a new day.
> CBRS 6/90, KR 3/1/90

Andrews, Sylvia. *Rattlebone Rock*. HarperCollins, 1995. Illustrator: Jennifer Plecas. Grades K-1
> People are attracted to the music in the graveyard created by the skeletons and ghosts. This is a good story to share aloud, allowing listeners to join in with the "Booma-Boom, Squeaka-Squeak and Eeeka-Eeek!"
> BL 09/15/95, SLJ 11/95

Arnold, Katya. *Baba Yaga: A Russian Folktale*. North-South, 1993. Illustrated by the author. Grades 2-4
> When Baba Yaga is hungry, all children need to beware! Tishka, a young man, is quick-witted enough to escape this fate, but the pictures (woodcuts) of the witch are scary. The longer text and intricate illustrations make this book perfect for older students.
> BL 10/01/93, LT 03/94

Arnold, Katya. *Baba Yaga & the Little Girl*. North-South, 1994. Illustrated by the author. Grades 2-4
> In a story similar to Joanna Cole's *Bony Legs*, a witch's dog, cat, gate, and tree help save a girl sent on an errand to the Baba Yaga's house. Once again, this tale is for the upper-level primary students, and it proves kindness can help in the worst situations.
> BL 04/15/94, SLJ 08/94

Ayres, Becky Hickox. *Matreshka*. Doubleday, 1992. Illustrator: Alexi Natcher. Grades 1-3
> A Baba Yaga story in which a girl named Kata receives a hand-carved wooden doll that saves her from becoming the witch's dinner. Marianna Mayer, Hiawyn Oram and Elizabeth Winthrop also wrote picture books of this story.
> BL 01/15/93, HBG Spring 1993

Benjamin, Alan. *The Slightly Scary Halloween Flap Book.* Golden Books, 1998. Illustrator: Doug Bowles. Kindergarten

This is a brightly colored book that has 50 flaps to delight the youngest readers. There is a small amount of text, and the costumes, bats, colors, and treats revealed will be enjoyed by those children who cannot yet read.

Reviews not available.

Bennett, Jill. *Teeny Tiny.* Putnam, 1986. Illustrator: Tomie dePaola. Grades K-1

As in *Tailypo* and *The Teeny-Tiny Woman*, a tiny bone is taken from a churchyard by a teeny tiny woman. That night she is troubled by an angry, tiny voice. Students will see the ghosts hiding in the pictures and will join in ("GIVE ME MY BONE!") as the voice becomes louder.

BL 04/01/86, HB 07/86

Berlan, Kathryn Hook. *Andrew's Amazing Monsters.* Atheneum, 1993. Illustrator: Maxie Chambliss. Grades K-3

Andrew uses magic crayons to make magical monsters. When he wishes one night to have a real party with them, the fun begins. The monsters come to life, meet him in his attic, and later return to sleep at Andrew's command.

BL 03/01/93, SLJ 10/93

Bodkin, Odds. *The Banshee Train.* Clarion, 1995. Illustrator: Ted Rose. Grades 1-4

Written as a true story, a train in Denver is saved from disaster by the banshee ghost of a previous wreck. This is a heart-racing tale that brings the reader into the story and includes an author's note at the end.

BL 06/01/95, SLJ 08/95

Bodkin, Odds. *Ghost of the Southern Belle.* Little Brown, 1999. Illustrator: Bernie Fuchs. Grades 2-5

After the ship of a Confederate captain goes down, the ghost of the vessel returns, bringing death to all that race it. A young boy holds the deceased captain's good luck charm and ends the reign of sea terror.

BL 9/15/99, SLJ 9/99

Brown, Marc. *Arthur's Halloween.* Little Brown, 1982. Illustrated by the author. Grades K-2 🎥

This is a popular story for Halloween, and is still in print due to the PBS show. The costumes, houses, and general creepiness of Halloween scare Arthur. When he meets Mrs. Tibble in her spooky house, his fears subside.

Reviews not available.

Brown, Ruth. *A Dark, Dark Tale.* Dial, 1981. Illustrated by the author. Grades K-2 🎥

A cat takes a spooky journey in a dark, dark house up a dark, dark stairway until he

frightens a mouse "in a dark, dark box of a dark, dark corner of a dark, dark cupboard in the dark, dark room." The illustrations are eerie, particularly one of abandoned toys that seem to have a mind of their own.

SLJ 01/82, NYTBR 11/81

Brown, Ruth. *One Stormy Night.* Dutton, 1992. Illustrated by the author. Grades K-1

You just can't go wrong with Ruth Brown, and this book is no exception. The illustrations show a dog wandering on a stormy night. The dog encounters several animals before moving on to his resting spot in a shivery surprise ending.

BL 8/93, SLJ 9/93

Brusca, Maria Cristina, and Tona Wilson. *The Blacksmith and the Devils.* Henry Holt, 1992. Illustrator: Maria Cristina Brusca. Grades 3-6

This is the Argentinean version of *Wicked Jack and the Devil*, in which the devil offers Pobreza gold and youth for his soul. Three times Lucifer (as named in this text) is tricked, and finally he relinquishes Pobreza from his commitment. Not able to enter heaven, Pobreza wanders the earth, triggering poverty out on the pampas.

KR 09/15/92, HBG Fall 1991

Buehner, Caralyn. *A Job for Wittilda.* Dial, 1993. Illustrator: Mark Buehner. Grades K-2

Wittilda is the funkiest witch in town, and she has a soft spot for homeless cats. When 47 tummies start growling, she is forced to find a job and discovers that she is exceptional at delivering pizza. Bright pictures with hidden spiders and mice will intrigue children.

BL 07/93, LT 11/93

Bunting, Eve. *Ghost's Hour, Spook's Hour.* Clarion, 1987. Illustrator: Donald Carrick. Grades K-1

Of course it's scary during stormy weather, especially late at night with no electricity. This book is written well for participatory sharing; for example, "Woooo outside my window," and "My bedroom door moaned …Eeeeeee."

BL 08/87, SLJ 09/87

Bunting, Eve. *I am the Mummy Heb-Nefert.* Harcourt Brace, 1997. Illustrator: David Christiana. Grades 3-6

The title says it all. Heb-Nefert is an Egyptian woman now mummified. As she looks out at the museum-goers, she remembers her life, customs, clothing, and activities, all of which are woven into the story. For older readers.

HBG Fall 1997, SLJ 08/97

Bunting, Eve. *In the Haunted House.* Clarion, 1990. Illustrator: Susan Meddaugh. Grades K-1

Two pairs of unidentified feet are walking through a house, haunted by all sorts of horrible creatures. The rhyming text moves them along, and on the last page, readers see a father and daughter emerging from a Halloween attraction.

HB 11/90, LT 05/91

Bunting, Eve. *Night of the Gargoyles.* Clarion, 1994. Illustrator: David Wiesner. Grades 3-6

Stone gargoyles come to life at night, peering into windows and watching the museum displays. The illustrations are dark, and reveal the true essence of the grotesque figures. The poetic text is hardly a story, nor is it scary, but the combination of the pictures and verse produces an eerie effect.

BL 10/01/94, LT 01/95

Bunting, Eve. *Scary, Scary Halloween.* Clarion, 1986. Illustrator: Jan Brett. Grades K-1

A mother cat is scared for herself and her kittens as she watches trick-or-treaters. The story is told in rhyme, and the illustrations are bold. In the end, the cats themselves go out and scare some mice.

HB 11/86, SLJ 12/86

Carlson, Natalie Savage. *Spooky and the Witch's Goat.* Lothrop, Lee & Shepard, 1989. Illustrator: Andrew Glass. Grades K-1

A hungry goat leads Spooky and Snowball to a witch's house, where they see her cast a spell that throws the goat into the sky. This story provides an explanation for the goat constellation, Capricorn.

BL 3/1/89, SLJ 6/89

Carlstrom, Nancy White. *What a Scare, Jesse Bear.* Simon & Schuster, 1999. Illustrator: Bruce Degen. Grades K-1

Jesse Bear has fun and enjoys Halloween by picking out a pumpkin, making a jack-o'-lantern, wearing a costume, and going trick-or-treating.

BL 09/01/99, SLJ 10/99

Carter, David A. *In a Dark, Dark Wood.* Simon & Schuster, 1991. Illustrated by the author. Grades K-2

This is the traditional story ("In a dark, dark wood there was a dark, dark house....") with a twist. In the dark, dark box on the dark, dark shelf there is...a ghost! The ghost is a pop-up that springs at the reader with a surprising flap.

HBG Spring 1992, LT 05/92

Cole, Joanna. *Bony-Legs.* Four Winds, 1983. Illustrator: Dirk Zimmer. Grades K-3 📼

The witch (similar to a Baba Yaga, but not named as one) has Sasha, and she wants to eat her. Sasha escapes with the help of the cat, dog, and gate, who have given her magical gifts in return for her kindness.

HB 02/84, SLJ 12/83

Cooney, Nancy Evans. *Go Away Monsters, Lickety Split.* Putnam, 1990. Illustrator: Maxie Chambliss. Kindergarten

When the reality of the new, big house sets in, Jeffrey has a hard time sleeping at night.

His mother buys him a new kitty named Lickety, who sleeps on his bed and eases his fear of the dark.

CBRS 08/90, LA 03/91

Crebbin, June. *Into the Castle*. Candlewick, 1996. Illustrator: John Bendall-Brunello. Grades K-1

Told in lighthearted rhyming text, this is the story of five friends touring an old castle to see if the legendary monster really does live inside. They see spooky shadows and a creepy dungeon, but little do they know that the monster is waiting to be released.

BL 8/96, HBG Fall 1996

cummings, e.e. *hist whist*. Crown, 1989. Illustrator: Deborah Kogan Ray. Grades 1-5

This is the original poem of e.e. cummings, which simply brings forth witches, goblins, ghosts, and the devil. The illustrations are deep, murky, and mysterious.

HB 11/89, LT 03/90

DeFelice, Cynthia. *Cold Feet*. DK Ink, 2000. Illustrator: Robert Andrew Parker. Grades 2-6

Not necessarily scary, but definitely twisted, this traditional Scottish folktale shows Willie McPhee as a traveling bagpiper. He doesn't do well, and poverty forces him to walk nearly shoeless. He exchanges "boots" with a frozen, dead man, but gets more than he bargained for—feet. With the feet, he plays a trick, but the last laugh may be on Willie.

BL 9/1/00, SLJ 9/00

DeFelice, Cynthia. *The Dancing Skeleton*. Macmillan, 1989. Illustrator: Robert Andrew Parker. Grades K-6

This is a perfect retelling of the Southern folktale in which a dead man won't rest. After dancing his crusty bones to the floor, Aaron's skeleton snaps its yellow teeth and howls, "OOOOOO-WHEEEE! AIN'T WE HAVIN' FUN?"

HBG 07/89, LT 05/90

DeFelice, Cynthia. *Willy's Silly Grandma*. Orchard, 1997. Illustrator: Shelley Jackson. Grades 1-4

When it comes to superstitions, Willy's grandma knows what she knows. The illustration of the bogeyman makes this book scary as Willy finds out the hard way that his Grandma and her superstitions are not so silly after all.

KR 3/01/97, SLJ 04/97

Del Negro, Janice. *Lucy Dove*. DK Ink, 1998. Illustrator: Leonid Gore. Grades 2-6

In this story, based on a Celtic tale, a seamstress sets her heart on a gold reward offered by a superstitious laird. She must sew him trousers by the light of a full moon in a haunted cemetery. As she sets to work, a fearsome bogle emerges from the earth, hungering for "blood and marrow, marrow and blood."

BL 09/01/98, HBG Fall 1998

Demarest, Chris. *Morton and Sidney*. Macmillan, 1987. Illustrated by the author. Kindergarten

There are so many monsters in Morton's closet that the boy must help Sidney, a monster who's been kicked out, return to his rightful spot. The two join forces to trick the other monsters, and in the end, everyone is satisfied.

BL 05/15/87, SLJ 04/87

Dickens, Charles. *Captain Murderer*. Adapted by George Harland. Lothrop, Lee & Shepard, 1986. Illustrator: Rown Barne-Murphy. Grade 6 & Up

I'm not sure that I would use this story as a picture book as the size is small, and the illustrations do not add much to the vivid retelling of Dickens's wife-chopping tale. I would use the book as a short read-aloud for older students because the retelling is concise and horrific.

KR 7/15/86

Diviny, Sean. *Halloween Motel*. HarperCollins, 2000. Illustrator: Joe Rocco. Grades K-2

This is a book for goofy, ghoul-loving children. Simple rhymes, garish cartoon illustrations, and bad jokes lead the reader through hotel rooms of shrieking witches and groaning mummies.

BL 9/1/00, SLJ 9/00

Donaldson, Julia. *The Gruffalo*. Dial, 1999. Illustrator: Axel Scheffler. Grades K-1

A tiny mouse makes his way through the woods. He thwarts a hungry fox, owl, and snake by warning them of the ferocious monster, "The Gruffalo." When the monster actually appears, the mouse creates another story to save himself once more.

KR 06/99

Donnelly, Liza. *Dinosaurs' Halloween*. Scholastic, 1987. Illustrated by the author. Grades K-1

A boy and his dog dress up as dinosaurs for Halloween, and along the way they come across another trick-or-treater in a dinosaur mask. When bullies try to steal candy, masks are ripped off, revealing one trick-or-treater who truly is a dinosaur.

BL 12/15/87, SLJ 03/88

Drescher, Henrik. *The Boy Who Ate Around*. Hyperion, 1994. Illustrated by the author. Grades K-2

This book is a little twisted, though not scary in nature. It is the story of Mo, a boy trying to get out of eating his disgusting dinner. He turns himself into a monster, eats everything in the world (including his mother, father, and teachers), and finds himself lonely enough to try eating that same plate of food he rejected.

BL 11/01/9 01/95

Duquennoy, Jacques. *The Ghosts in the Cellar*. Harcourt, 1996. Illustrated by the author. Grades K-3

Four easily frightened ghosts search their house to uncover the source of loud, booming noises. They find their Aunt Gigi, who's been locked in a trunk for 500 years, and celebrate her birthday.

Reviews not available

Duquennoy, Jacques. *The Ghosts' Trip to Loch Ness.* Harcourt, 1996. Illustrated by the author. Grades K-1

Four ghosts take a trip to Loch Ness in the hope of seeing the monster. Playfully, the monster hides from them, but when they return home and develop their pictures, they see how close to the monster they were.

HBG Spring 1997, SLJ 10/96

Emberley, Ed. *Go Away, Big Green Monster!* Little Brown, 1992. Illustrated by the author. Kindergarten

This book is designed with cutouts so that with each page turn the monster appears and then disappears. Page by page, the body parts are added, and then later removed, until all that is seen are the two yellow eyes.

BL 04/15/93, SLJ 07/93

Enderle, Judith Ross and Stephanie Gordon Tessler. *Six Creepy Sheep.* Boyds Mill, 1992. Illustrator: John O'Brien. Grades K-1

One by one, five of the six sheep run to escape other trick-or-treaters dressed in spooky costumes. The final sheep searches, and finds everyone (including the scary neighbors) safe and happy at a Halloween party.

HB 03/93, SLJ 10/92

Fox, Mem. *Guess What?* Harcourt Brace, 1990. Illustrator: Vivienne Goodman. Grades K-1

"Far away from here lives a crazy lady called Daisy O'Grady." This is followed by simple questions ("Is she tall? Guess!"), which are answered with each page turn ("YES!"). The illustrations border on bizarre but can be appreciated by more sophisticated audiences.

HBG 07/90, SLJ 11/90

Glassman, Peter. *My Working Mom.* Morrow, 1994. Illustrator: Tedd Arnold. Grades K-3

The narrator does not reveal what his mom's job is although we know she has good days and bad, like any other employed mom. At the end of the story, the pictures indicate her profession—a witch!

HBG Fall 1994, SLJ 08/94

Graves, Keith. *Frank Was a Monster.* Chronicle, 1999. Illustrated by the author. Grades K-4

A Frankenstein monster with a green head and jointed body parts decides he belongs onstage, dancing. As he moves about, his head unzips, his brains spill out, and his body dismantles to the audience's disgust.

BL 7/99, SLJ 7/99

Greene, Carol. *The Thirteen Days of Halloween.* Troll, 2000. Illustrator: Tim Raglin. Grades K-3

Reissued from 1983, this is the song *The Twelve Days of Christmas*, Halloween style. The gifts received are bats, worms, spiders, and the other Halloween treats. Use with *The Thirteen*

Hours of Halloween (Regan) and you can sing all day.
BL 9/1/00

Guthrie, Donna. *The Witch Has an Itch*. Little Simon, 1990. Illustrator: Katy Arnsteen.
Grades K-3

The worst witch in ages, Gromelda (who's mean enough to topple ice cream cones and make it rain on Saturday), gets an itch. She goes to a wizard for help, only to have him diagnose her ailment: She is allergic to evil magic.
Reviews not available.

Hancock, Sibyl. *Esteban and the Ghost*. Dial, 1983. Illustrator: Dirk Zimmer. Grades 2-5

Although this is an old story, it seems to be in most libraries. Similar to the character in "The Strange Visitor," and "The Tinker and the Ghost," Esteban endures a full night at a haunted castle and helps a dismembered ghost that drops bit by bit from the fireplace. He is rewarded for his efforts with the ghost's gold.
SLJ 11/83

Harness, Cheryl. *Midnight in the Cemetery: A Spooky Search-and-Find Alphabet Book*.
Simon & Schuster, 1999. Illustrator: Robin Brickman. Grades 2-6

In rhyming text, children walk through a cemetery and disturb the ghosts, who later have a "spiritual" party. The reader is expected to search each page to determine items that begin with the correlating letters of the alphabet. This is not an easy task, even for the creators.
Reviews not available.

Hearn, Diane Dawson. *Bad Luck Boswell*. Simon & Schuster, 1995. Illustrated by the author.
Grades K-1

Boswell is a black cat, and although he does cause a *bit* of bad luck, he is unjustly cast from the town by the superstitious villagers. A witch finds him, and plans to use him in a horrible potion to curse the villagers, but Boswell stops the spell, and changes his own luck in the process.
CBRS Winter 1996, HBG Spring 1996

Heide, Florence Parry. *Some Things Are Scary*. Candlewick, 2000. Illustrator: Jules Feiffer.
Grades K-2

This book shares scary things that are worse than any monster under the bed—like getting hugged by somebody you don't like or finding out that your best friend has a best friend who isn't you. This humorous book can be used to discuss fears.
BL 10/15/00, CCB-B 12/1/00

Heinz, Brian J. *The Monsters' Test*. Millbrook, 1996. Illustrator: Sal Murdocca. Grades 2-4

In somewhat advanced rhyme, monsters in a castle compete on Halloween night to determine who is the scariest. The contest does not produce a winner, for trick-or-treaters

frighten the beasties away. The last page provides a mirror and asks the reader to decide if he or she is the scariest.

CBRS 11/96, SLJ 10/96

Hendra, Sue. *Scary Party*. Candlewick, 1998. Illustrated by the author. Kindergarten

A simple, rhythmical book that progresses through various body parts in this manner: "Heads, heads, look at the heads, dancing in the dark. OH NO!" At the end of the book a trick-or-treat party is revealed, which is not so scary after all.

PW 09/28/98

Hill, Susan. *Beware, Beware*. Candlewick, 1993. Illustrator: Angela Barrett. Grades K-2

In poetic, sparse text, we follow a young girl from her mother's cozy kitchen into the woods. Her imagination grows with the illustrations; eyes, goblins, and fierce animals can be seen in the trees. When she finally turns, she finds her mother, and the safety is a welcome change.

BL 11/15/93, SLJ 2/94

Hines, Anna Grossnickle. *When the Goblins Came Knocking*. Greenwillow, 1995. Illustrated by the author. Grades K-1

A young boy remembers how frightened he was of the costumes he saw last Halloween. This year, he is determined not to be scared; instead, he wears his own costume, a masterpiece.

PW 09/18/95, HBG Spring 1996

Hoban, Russell. *Monsters*. Scholastic, 1989. Illustrator: Quentin Blake. Grades K-2

John's parents worry about him due to his unhealthy obsession with drawing monsters. They schedule a meeting with his art teacher, and then bring the boy to a doctor, who asks John to complete a larger-than-life drawing of his current monster. The monster, upon completion, eats the doctor, but John is…well, fine.

BL 9/1/90, SLJ 10/90

Holabird, Katherine. *Angelina's Halloween*. Pleasant Company Publishing, 2000. Illustrator: Helen Craig. Grades K-2

Because she can't wear a firefly costume, Angelina's younger sister Polly dresses as a ghost for Halloween. The costume is deceiving, and mixed identities behind the outfit give everyone a scare.

PW 9/25/00

Howe, James. *Scared Silly: A Halloween Treat*. Morrow, 1989. Illustrator: Leslie Morrill. Grades 1-2

On Halloween night, the pets of the Monroe family (Bunnicula included) are spooked by a witch. Who is she, they fear, and will she cast some type of horrible spell? Of course not; she's

part of the family, simply wearing a Halloween costume.
    BL 08/89, SLJ 08/89

Hubbard, Patricia. *Trick-or-Treat Countdown.* Holiday House, 1998. Illustrator: Michael Letzig.
  Kindergarten
    A bright, bold counting book, in which readers encounter typical Halloween sights.
Rhyming text, sound effects, and reassurances blend together so that nobody is scared:
"Werewolves, bats, and monsters mean, All make-believe on Halloween."
    BL 09/01/98, SLJ 09/98

Huck, Charlotte. *Creepy Countdown.* Greenwillow, 1998. Illustrator: Joseph Smith. Grades K-1
    Ten mice spook the scarecrow, cats, ghosts, and other creepy critters out of their resting
places, while the reader ascends in counting to 10. The ghouls are then spooked again, in
descending order, until all are back to their original starting places.
    BL 9/1/98, SLJ 9/98

Hulme, Joy N. *Eerie Feary Feeling: A Hairy Scary Pop-up Book.* Orchard, 1998. Illustrator:
  Paul Ely. Grades K-2
    In simple rhyming text, this book shows three-dimensional "eerie feary" goblins, "hairy
scary" owls, a "spooky kooky" cauldron, and "quaky shaky" ghosts.
    CBW 10/11/98, SLJ 12/98

Hutchins, Pat. *The Very Worst Monster.* Greenwillow, 1985. Illustrated by the author.
  Grades K-1
    Hazel's younger monster brother Billy is doted on and expected to be "The Worst
Monster in the World." Hazel knows better, as she is a far worse monster than Billy. In the end,
Hazel proves that Billy can be only "The Worst *BABY* Monster in the World."
    KR 03/01/85, SLJ 05/85

Irving, Washington. *The Headless Horseman: A Retelling of Washington Irving's "The Legend
  of Sleepy Hollow."* Retold and illustrated by Emma Harding. 1995. Grades 3-5
    This is not the best version of the classic legend. It is darkly illustrated, and the charac-
ters don't have the New England visualizations that Irving depicted. In the retelling, the text is
watered down and seems flat.
    BL 12/01/95, HBG Spring 1996

Irving, Washington. *The Legend of Sleepy Hollow.* Retold and illustrated by Will Moses.
  Philomel, 1995. Grades 3-6
    Written in a comfortable style with language similar to a storyteller's, this book would be
enjoyed as a read-aloud. Although the text is lengthy, it is interspersed with illustrations that
share a fellow Hudson Valley inhabitant's viewpoint of Sleepy Hollow in the time of Irving's life.
    LT 09/95, PW 07/24/95

Irving, Washington. *The Legend of Sleepy Hollow.* Retold by Robert D. San Souci. Doubleday, 1986. Illustrator: Daniel San Souci. Grades 3-6

This retelling is completely appealing. The illustrations are large, and they enhance the story. The text is written in a style that would be well suited for a read-aloud or just right for the intermediate-aged readers.

BL 12/01/86, SLJ 12/86

Jackson, Jean. *Big Lips and Hairy Arms: A Monster Story.* DK Ink, 1998. Illustrator: Vera Rosenberry. Grades K-1

Thorndike and Nelson, two monster friends, are frightened when a prank caller says, "I have big lips and hairy arms, and I'm five blocks away." The calls keep coming as the monster gets closer, until it arrives and shows them what can be done with big lips (a kiss) and hairy arms (a hug).

BL 12/1/5/98, SLJ 10/98

Johnson, Paul Brett. *A Perfect Pork Stew.* Orchard, 1998. Illustrated by the author. Grades 2-4

A hybrid of Baba Yaga and Ivan the Fool, this humorous story was fashioned about the misunderstandings between a witch who needs glasses and a simple, clever boy. When Baba Yaga mistakes clumps of dirt for a pig in Ivan's cart, she tricks him into putting the "pig" in her soup pot. In the end, the trick is on her as Ivan walks off with a pig, and she eats dirt soup.

HBG Fall 1998

Johnston, Tony. *Alice Nizzy Nazzy: The Witch of Santa Fe.* Putnam, 1995. Illustrator: Tomie dePaola. Grades K-2

This is supposed to be a Baba Yaga story set in Santa Fe, but something about the text and illustrations do not add up. Alice Nizzy Nazzy is the witch, a mean woman with a reputation for eating children. Yet, when Manuela approaches her in search of her flock of sheep, the plot dissolves, with the witch abandoning Manuela because she tastes too sour. The cheerful illustrations do not add to the choppy text, and the overall outcome is ineffective.

BL 3/15/95, SLJ 4/95

Johnston, Tony. *The Ghost of Nicholas Greebe.* Dial, 1996. Illustrator: S. D. Schindler. Grades K-3

This is the tale of a dead man's bone that travels halfway around the world before returning to his grave 100 years later. The ghost of the man haunts his old house until, through good luck and mischievous dogs, his bone is returned to his body.

HB 11/96, SLJ 12/96

Johnston, Tony. *The Soup Bone.* Harcourt, 1990. Illustrator: Margot Tomes. Grades K-1

Ooops! While looking for a soup bone, a little old lady unearths a skeleton. She and the skeleton take turns scaring each other. Then, as friends, they decide to have fun spooking others on Halloween night.

BL 10/15/90, SLJ 01/91

Johnston, Tony. *Very Scary.* Harcourt Brace, 1995. Illustrator: Douglas Florian. Kindergarten

A large pumpkin sits in the moonlight and attracts an owl, a cat, crickets, and a witch before a group of children carve it into a very scary jack-o'-lantern. Rhythmical language is incorporated ("A witch came sneaky-sneaky-sneaky") and the text winds visually on the page.

BL 09/15/95, LT 09/95

Kamish, Daniel, and David Kamish. *The Night the Scary Beasties Popped out of My Head.* Random House, 1998. Grades K-1

Dan draws his nightmare beastie, and before he can erase it, the creature springs to life. Dan pursues the beastie on a six-legged dog he has drawn and finally ends the chase by drowning the nightmare in a shower.

PW 6/29/98, SLJ 11/98

Kellogg, Steven. *The Christmas Witch.* Dial, 1992. Illustrated by the author. Grades K-2

Gloria is not evil enough for the witch academy run by Madame Pestilence. After noticing an angel one evening, she is introduced to Christmas magic, and she converts to help those battling on the planet Pepperdoons. Gloria's kindness ends the feud and stops the Pestilence curse.

LT 11/92, SLJ 10/92

Khdir, Kate and Sue Nash. *Little Ghost.* Barron's, 1991. Illustrator: Caroline Church. Kindergarten

Little Ghost is not able to scare children, as he is too silly. His teacher, Miss Scarum sends him off, and he visits children performing a Halloween play. He becomes the star of the show and accomplishes his mission upon his return to school.

Reviews not available.

Kimmel, Eric. *Baba Yaga: A Russian Folktale.* Holiday House, 1991. Illustrator: Megan Lloyd. Grades K-2

When you have a horn growing out of your head, you aren't typically considered attractive, but Marina is a kind girl anyway. Her wicked stepmother sends her on an errand to the local witch's house where the girl's thoughtfulness saves her life and gives her physical beauty.

BL 05/01/91, SLJ 06/91

Kimmel, Eric. *Hershel and the Hanukkah Goblins.* Holiday House, 1985. Illustrator: Trina Schart Hyman. Grades 3-5

It's always good when you can add a spooky twist to a holiday other than Halloween. Goblins have destroyed all of the village Hanukkah celebrations, but Hershel uses his wits to defeat the hideous creatures and restore the celebration of light.

Larranaga, Ana Martin. *Woo! The Not-So-Scary Ghost.* Scholastic Press, 2000. Illustrated by the author. Kindergarten

Tired of the nagging from his family, Little Woo ghost floats away from home one morning. A farmer's wife mistakes him for a sheet, and he ends up in her washer, on her clothesline, and under her hot iron. His only escape is to squash his timidness, which he does in time to arrive home safely before dark.

BL 12/1/00, SLJ 9/00

Leedy, Loreen. *The Dragon Halloween Party*. Holiday House, 1986. Illustrated by the author. Grades 1-3

While the dragons prepare for a party, the story line is enhanced with short tips and recipes for a great Halloween.

SLJ 12/86

Leedy, Loreen. *The Monster Money Book*. Holiday House, 1992. Illustrated by the author. Grades 1-4

This book explains economic principles by discussing the necessity of dues for two new members of the Monster Club. Although the book is not scary and has very little plot, it may be appealing for teachers trying to teach themes such as scarcity, needs and wants, profit, and debt.

BL 3/15/92, SLJ 6/92

Leuck, Laura. *My Monster Mama Loves Me So*. Lothrop, Lee & Shepard, 1999. Illustrator: Mark Buehner. Grades K-1

In rhyming text, a triple-eyed monster shares how wonderful his mama is: "She helps me climb the jungle gym, takes me to the swamp to swim…." The illustrations are bright and full of fun, goofy monsters.

PW 09/27/99, SLJ 01/00

Levine, Arthur. *The Boy Who Drew Cats: A Japanese Folktale*. Dial, 1994. Illustrator: Frederic Clement. Grades 2-5

This is the traditional story of a boy who saves a Buddhist temple that has been abandoned due to a terrifying monster. The boy, an artist, wanders into the temple and draws cats on large screens. In the morning, he finds that the cats came to life and destroyed the goblin rat.

HBG Fall 1994, LT 03/95

Lewis, J. Patrick. *The House of Boo*. Atheneum, 1998. Illustrator: Katya Krenina. Grades K-2

This book is darkly illustrated, and written in a poetic style called a Rubaiyat. It tells of the night three children attempted to spy on old man Boo Scoggins but found nothing bur eerie sounds and shadows up on Humpback Hill.

Reviews not available.

Lindgren, Astrid. *The Ghost of Skinny Jack*. Viking, 1988. Illustrator: Ilon Wikland. Grades 2-4

A boy and girl are scared by their grandmother's tale of a wild young man who became

part of the undead. This picture book contains a lengthy amount of text. It is similar in story to *Lucy Dove* (Del Negro).

    BL 01/01/89, SLJ 03/89

Lodge, Bernard. *Mouldylocks*. Houghton Mifflin, 1998. Illustrated by the author. Grades K-3

    It is the birthday of Mouldylocks the witch, and her friends throw her a surprise birthday party. They play *Pass the Gargoyle, Bewitched Musical Chairs,* and *Snakes and Ladders,* before creating a spell and enjoying birthday cake.

    BL 9/1/98, SLJ 10/98

Loredo, Elizabeth. *Boogie Bones*. Putnam, 1997. Illustrator: Kevin Hawkes. Grades 1-4

    Boogie Bones, a skeleton with a love for dancing, dresses up in clothes for a dance contest. During a tango, he gets carried away, and the clothes fall off, revealing nothing but bones. Horrified, the townsfolk stand back until little Maggie Brown takes Boogie's hand, and the dance continues.

    BL 9/1/97, SLJ 9/97

Martin, Bill and John Archambault. *The Ghost-Eye Tree*. Holt, 1985. Illustrator: Ted Rand. Grades K-2

    A boy pretends not to be scared as he and his sister walk down a path past an old oak tree. The dark and the sounds play tricks with his mind, but his sister gets him through the Ghost-Eye Tree's attempt to scare him.

    BL 12/15/85, SLJ 02/86

Martin, Bill and John Archambault. *The Magic Pumpkin*. Holt, 1989. Illustrator: Robert J. Lee. Grades K-2

    A jack-o'-lantern promises to be the guard of a house and protects it from skunks and owls. When his fairy friends arrive, the pumpkin gets wild, spinning and dancing magically, and his light needs to be snuffed. Not a scary story, but one relating to the themes of Halloween.

    BL 09/01/89, LT 09/89

Martin, Bill, Jr. *Old Devil Wind*. Harcourt, 1993. Illustrator: Barry Root. Grades K-1

    This is a good book to use when you want children to join in. It is a cumulative tale that incorporates wailing, thumping, rattling, and swishing sounds in the setting of a creepy old house.

    BL 10/01/93, HB 01/94

Martin, Bill, Jr. *The Wizard*. Harcourt Brace, 1994. Illustrator: Alex Schaefer. Grades K-2

    "I loop the loop! I zipper-zoop! Poof! I disappear...." A wizard and his assistants bumble about a cauldron until the wizard himself disappears. Bright illustrations enhance the wizard's attempt to conjure a spell.

    BL 10/15/94, SLJ 02/95

Mayer, Marianna. *Baba Yaga and Vasilisa the Brave.* Morrow, 1994. Illustrator: K. Y. Craft. Grades 2-5

A doll helps a sweet girl escape death by completing the tasks demanded by the evil Baba Yaga. The illustrations are lush with elaborate details and borders, and Baba Yaga is gruesome. As a weathered ghoul, she is seen with a pipe and the caption "Smoking after meals is one of Baba Yaga's many bad habits."

BL 06/01/94, SLJ 07/94

Mayer, Mercer. *There's a Nightmare in My Closet.* Dial, 1968. Illustrated by the author. Kindergarten

This is the classic tale in which a boy decides to eliminate the nightmare in his closet. When he does, with his toy gun, he sees what a truly terrible nightmare he has: a monster with a horrible head and huge teeth, but a timid heart.

Reviews not available.

McBratney, Sam. *The Dark at the Top of the Stairs.* Candlewick, 1996. Illustrator: Ivan Bates. Grades K-1

This is a silly book that deals with the element of fear that is so common in young children. Baby mice are curious, yet terrified, at the thought of the monster that lives at the top of the stairs. This book is good for a bedtime story with little ones who scare easily.

BL 01/01/97, HBG Fall 1996

McDonald, Megan. *The Bone Keeper.* DK Ink., 1999. Illustrator: Brian Karas. Grades 2-6

"Some say Bone Woman brings the dead back to life." The Bone Keeper searches the sand of the desert for bones, and each piece she finds she pieces together. In this book, she constructs a wolf that leaps off howling in the night.

BL 04/15/99, SLJ 05/99

Medearis, Angela Shelf. *The Ghost of Sifty Sifty Sam.* Scholastic Press, 1997. Illustrator: Jacqueline Rogers. Grades 2-5

Dan is a chef who cooks the best fish in Texas. Sam is a hungry ghost with an appetite for fright. When Dan spends the night at Sam's haunted house, the two make a deal that provides well for both of them.

BL 12/1/97, SLJ 11/97

Meddaugh, Susan. *The Witches' Supermarket.* Houghton Mifflin, 1991. Illustrated by the author. Grades 1-3

This is a story of Martha, the famous talking dog, written before she acquired her ability to talk. Martha and Helen dress up for Halloween (Martha as a cat, Helen a witch) and use their wits to escape from a supermarket full of witches.

BL 08/91, KR 08/15/91

Merriam, Eve. *Halloween ABC.* Macmillan, 1987. Illustrator: Lane Smith. Grades 3-4

This book has some sophisticated poems (for example, **D**, DEMON) in which the text delves into demons and their dance with Satan, Mephistopheles, Lucifer, and Beelzebub. Younger students may not understand it, but older readers will appreciate it.

BL 10/15/87, KR 08/01/87

Milich, Melissa. *Can't Scare Me!* Doubleday, 1995. Illustrator: Tyrone Geter. Grades 1-3

The ghost stories seem like fun until somebody gets scared. Young Eugenia must walk Mr. Munroe home after he hears too much on a spooky night.

BL 01/01/95, SLJ 04/95

Miller, William. *The Conjure Woman.* Atheneum, 1996. Illustrator: Terea D. Shaffer. Grades 2-4

A conjure woman named Madame Zina cures a sick boy by tying herbs around his neck, drawing a circle, and then flying the two of them back to Africa in a dreamlike state. There, the natives perform rituals and give medicines until the boy feels strong enough to return home. While this is not a scary story, conjure women often are associated with witchcraft.

BL 2/1/5/96, SLJ 3/96

Namm, Diane. *Monsters!* Children's Press, 1990. Illustrator: Maxie Chambliss. Kindergarten

A "My First Reader" picture book with friendly monsters that show up around a boy's room as he prepares for bed. He knows they are there although they try to hide, and the final picture shows the monsters as the stuffed animals they truly are.

BL 02/01/91

Nikola-Lisa, W. *Shake Dem Halloween Bones.* Houghton Mifflin, 1997. Illustrator: Mike Reed. Grades K-2

This is possibly the grooviest, most rhythmical book to share on this list. It follows a prowling cat throughout a city on Halloween night. One by one, the coolest fairy tale characters join in a celebration where they "shake, shake, shake dem bones now," at the Halloween ball.

BL 10/1/97, CCB-B 12/97

Nimmo, Jenny. *The Witches and the Singing Mice.* Dial, 1993. Illustrator: Angela Barrett. Grades 1-4

Two Scottish cats witness three witches casting spells on village children. Only Old Granny Pine can help them.

BL 08/93, SLJ 08/93

Numeroff, Laura. *Monster Munchies.* Random Beginner Books, 1998. Illustrator: Nate Evans. Grades K-2

Told in rhyme, this counting book (1 through 20) describes the habits and actions of assorted monsters. For example, "One giant monster wears a dress, eats a couch, and makes a mess."

CBW 12/98

O'Connell, Jennifer. *Ten Timid Ghosts*. Scholastic, 2000. Illustrated by the author. Grades K-1

"Ten timid ghosts in a haunted house – a witch moved in, and wanted them out." So goes the premise for this text, where the ten ghosts leave in fear, and then grow angry and strike back.

Reviews not available.

Ogburn, Jacqueline K. *Scarlett Angelina Wolverton-Manning*. Dial, 1994. Illustrator: Brian Ajhar. Grades 2-5

Kidnapped for ransom, Scarlett tries to warn her oppressor to free her, but he must learn his lesson the hard way as the full moon begins to rise. Cartoon illustrations keep the mood light and mischievous.

BL 11/1/5/94, SLJ 11/94

O'Keefe, Susan. *One Hungry Monster: A Counting Book in Rhyme*. Joy Street/Little, Brown, 1989. Illustrator: Lynn Munsinger. Kindergarten

Told in rhyming text ("One hungry monster underneath my bed, moaning and groaning and begging to be fed."), this is the story of a boy who carries food to ten monsters, including 7 roasted turkeys, 9 watermelons, and more.

BL 06/01/89, SLJ 07/89

O'Malley, Kevin. *Velcome*. Walker, 1997. Illustrated by the author. Grades K-2

This picture book has four of the silliest scary stories ever to be told. The illustrations are hilarious (arrows through the head), and the story "The Didja" has been a hit with the first graders for years.

BL 09/01/97, SLJ 09/97

Oram, Hiawyn. *Baba Yaga and the Wise Doll*. Dutton, 1998. Illustrator: Ruth Brown. Grades K-6

Sent to the woods by her "Horrid" sisters, "Too Nice Child" is nearly tidbits for the gruesome Baba Yaga's toads. A doll in her pocket, a gift from her mother, helps Too Nice escape from becoming dinner as Baba Yaga tests her with various tasks.

BL 01/01/98, HB Spring 1998

Park, Barbara. *Psssst! It's Me…the Bogeyman*. Atheneum, 1998. Illustrator: Stephen Kroninger. Grades K-1

The Bogeyman makes an appeal to a boy in his bed. With Park's sharp humor, the "B man" explains what he does and does NOT do, as misprinted in a newspaper. The boy finally rids himself of the pest by inundating him with smelly socks on the floor.

BL 8/9/8, SLJ 9/98

Passan, Lisa. *Attack of the 50-Foot Teacher*. Holt, 2000. Illustrated by the author. Grades K-5

Miss Irma Birmbaum is the cruelest teacher in the school; she assigns homework on Halloween! On her way home, she encounters a UFO and is transformed into a 50-foot crea-

ture. She goes around scaring children until she realizes the fun of Halloween.
BL 11/15/00

Patschke, Steve. *The Spooky Book.* Walker, 1999. Illustrator: Matthew McElligott. Grades K-2
A boy and his new neighbor meet, each holding a copy of *The Spooky Book*. While they are reading *The Spooky Book*, the story begins to take place in real life.
SLJ 11/99, CBRS 10/99

Paul, Korky and Valerie Thomas. *Winnie the Witch.* Kane Miller, 1987. Illustrator: Korky Paul. Grades K-2
Winnie's black cat is difficult to see in her dark house. She continually mistakes him for furniture until she zaps him into rainbow shades. When the cat refuses to come out of hiding, Winnie changes the color scheme of her house and once again has a happy black cat.
Reviews not available.

Pitre, Felix. *Pace and the Witch: A Puerto Rican Folktale.* Lodestar, 1995. Illustrator: Christy Hale. Grades K-3
With an author's note and glossary to define Spanish words, this is a Rumpelstiltskin-type tale of a boy tricked by a witch. He learns her name from a crab, which then scuttles about the earth for fear of the witch's repercussions.
BL 05/15/95, SLJ 08/95

Reeves, Howard. *There Was an Old Witch.* Hyperion, 1998. Illustrator: David Catrow. Grades K-3
Following the song, "I Know an Old Lady," this witch unearths a mummy, conjures a haunt, and assembles a skeleton in her pursuit of a perfect hat adornment.
BL 12/1/5/98, SLJ 3/99

Reeves, Mona Rabun. *The Spooky Eerie Night Noise.* Bradbury, 1989. Illustrator: Paul Yalowitz. Grades K-1
Something is making terrible noises outside, frightening the child in the house. The family questions one another; could it be a tiger, a gremlin, a werewolf? No, they find out, it's just two skunks!
BL 08/89, SLJ 09/8

Regan, Dian. *Thirteen Hours of Halloween.* Albert Whitman, 1993. Illustrator: Lieve Baeten. Grades K-3
"In the first hour of Halloween my best friend gave to me a vulture in a dead tree." And, so it goes with mummies, goblins, werewolves, and more until the little girl gives away her gifts at the 13th hour.
HBG Spring 1994, SLJ 02/94

Roberts, Bethany. *Halloween Mice!* Clarion, 1995. Illustrator: Doug Cushman. Grades K-1
The mice are having a great Halloween party until a cat threatens to ruin it. The critters

create "a scary monster" with shadows, and it is just enough to frighten the cat. The rhyming text is fun for participation, "Having a party! *Whirl, whirl!* Faster! Faster! *Whish, whish!"*
 BL 01/15/95, LT 09/95

Robins, Arthur. *The Teeny Tiny Woman: A Traditional Tale.* Candlewick, 1998. Grades K-1
 The time-honored story of the woman with the tiniest voice, who takes the tiniest bone, which causes the tiniest problem, until she tells the owner, "TAKE IT!"
 BL 12/1/5/98, SLJ 9/98

Rosenberg, Liz. *Monster Mama.* Philomel, 1993. Illustrator: Stephen Gammel. Grades K-1
 Patrick's mother is a monster, but she loves her son Patrick. She raises him properly, teaching him to use his magic only for good. But one day, after three bullies steal his strawberry dessert, Patrick's mama shows everyone who's boss.
 BL 01/15/93, HB 03/93

Rosner, Ruth. *Nattie Witch.* Harper & Row, 1989. Illustrated by the author. Grades K-1
 After we see her breakfast of newt-loops and her school for witches, we realize just how different Nattie is. An ordinary day is never ordinary for a child who is a witch.
 HBG 08/89, SLJ 01/90

Roth, Susan L. *Night-Time Numbers: A Scary Counting Book.* Barefoot Books, 1999. Illustrated by the author. Kindergarten
 The question, "Who can you see?" is followed with different spooky answers ("One monster," "Nine spiders"). The last page includes an angel that is seen, "to keep me safe and sound." Illustrations are done in collage.
 KR 10/01/99, SLJ 10/99

Samton, Sheila. *Ten Tiny Monsters: A Superbly Scary Story of Subtraction.* Crown, 1997. Grades 1-2
 The ten monsters must scare off tinier creatures, or they won't make the monster team. As each one fails, they are bumped down a hill until the last monster feels lonely and eventually joins the others.
 SLJ 12/97

San Souci, Robert D. *The Boy and the Ghost.* Simon & Schuster, 1989. Illustrator: Brian Pinkney. Grades K-3
 A poor boy hopes to win a fortune for himself and his family by spending the night in a haunted house. Much like the character in the story *Esteban and the Ghost* (Hancock), he stands up to a frightening ghost whose body parts dangle bit by bit.
 BL 02/01/90, LT 03/90

San Souci, Robert D. *Cinderella Skeleton.* Harcourt, 2000. Illustrator: David Catrow. Grades 2-5
 This rhyming version of Cinderella sports a cemetery, a funeral wagon and a foot that

breaks off with a *snap!* Catrow, known for his political cartoons, adds a humorous and ghoulish touch.

BL 9/1/00, SLJ 9/00

San Souci, Robert D. *The Hobyahs.* Doubleday, 1994. Illustrator: Alexi Natchev. Grades 2-4

In this softer retelling of the original tale (no chopping of the dog's legs and head), the family's canines try to protect their owners from the goblins that want to eat them.

BL 02/01/94, SLJ 04/94

Sendak, Maurice. *Where the Wild Things Are.* Harper & Row, 1963. Illustrated by the author. Kindergarten

These are the most memorable monsters on the planet. I don't consider this classic story to be scary (a boy plays with imaginary monsters after being punished in his room), but some children find the monsters frightening.

Reviews not available.

Shaw, Nancy. *Sheep Trick-or-Treat.* Houghton Mifflin, 1997. Illustrator: Margot Apple. Grades K-1

The illustrations in this book are very funny, as sheep dress in costumes for Halloween trick-or-treating. Mummy sheep, rolled in gauze, join vampire and ape sheep to get clover and other treats. Their costumes come in handy when they see wolves nearby.

BL 9/1/97, SLJ 9/97

Shute, Linda. *Halloween Party.* Lothrop, 1994. Illustrated by the author. Grades K-2

At the end of a Halloween party, the guests remove their masks. It is then that they discover two guests, a witch and a vampire boy, are not using masks.

KR 08/15/94, SLJ 09/94

Sierra, Judy. *The House That Drac Built.* Harcourt, Brace, 1995. Illustrator: Will Hillenbrand. Grades K-2

"This is the house that Drac built." The reader is brought through the spooky house, complete with a zombie, monster, mummy, manticore, werewolf, cat, bat and fiend. Once revealed, the creatures then are soothed by Halloween trick-or-treaters.

BL 09/15/95, LT 09/95

Sierra, Judy. *Wiley and the Hairy Man.* Dutton, 1996. Illustrator: Brian Pinkney. Grades K-4

In this traditional folktale, Wiley must escape the clutches of the conjure man, something that his father was not able to do. Wiley's dogs and his mother help him, and their trickery sends the conjure man away forever.

BL 03/01/96, SLJ 03/96

Silverman, Erica. *Big Pumpkin.* Macmillan, 1992. Illustrator: S.D. Schindler. Grades K-2 📼

Like the traditional story of "The Enormous Turnip," a big pumpkin cannot be removed

from the vine without the help of a ghost, a vampire, a mummy, and a bat. Everyone celebrates with pumpkin pie.

    BL 09/01/92, LT 09/92

Silverman, Erica. *The Halloween House*. Farrar, 1997. Illustrator: Jon Agee. Grades K-2

    When two prison escapees search for a house to spend the night, they never expect the house, complete with ghosts and skeletons, to be scarier than jail. They flee for the safety of their cell.

    BL 09/01/97, SLJ 11/97

Smith, Maggie. *There's a Witch Under the Stairs*. Lothrop, Lee & Shepard, 1991. Illustrated by the author. Grades K-1

    Frances knows a witch lives under her stairs, but try as she may, she cannot get rid of it. When Ellie, her stuffed elephant, is trapped with the witch, Frances rescues her and sends the witch packing.

    Reviews not available.

Steig, William. *Wizzil*. Farrar, 2000. Illustrator: Quentin Blake. Grades K-2

    Bored with her life, Wizzil the witch decides to torment the neighbors. Transforming herself into a bewitched glove, she annoys DeWitt Frimp until, in total disgust, he heaves the glove into the water. Wizzil nearly drowns, but DeWitt saves her.

    BL 10/1/00, SLJ 8/00

Stevenson, James. *Emma*. Greenwillow, 1985. Illustrated by the author. Grades K-2

    Emma needs flying lessons, but her wicked witch neighbors will not comply. She tricks them into believing she has mastered the flying technique, and then thanks her animal friends and assistants.

    KR 3/1/85, SLJ 4/85

Stevenson, James. *What's Under My Bed?* Greenwillow, 1983. Illustrated by the author. Grades K-2

    When his grandchildren can't sleep, Grandpa tells about his own childhood and the bedtime fears he experienced. The howling wind, creaky noises, and terrifying hoots all become clear in the end.

    HB 12/83, SLJ 12/83

Stutson, Caroline. *By the Light of the Halloween Moon*. Lothrop, 1993. Illustrator: Kevin Hawke. Grades K-2

    In this rhythmical text, a girl playing the violin attracts creepy listeners. The reader sees only her feet as a cat, bat, witch, and ghouls bumble about, trying to get a bite. She finally delivers a swat that sends them all scattering.

    BL 07/93, LT 05/94

Thomas, Frances. *What If?* Hyperion, 1998. Illustrator: Ross Collins. Kindergarten

A young monster's fears are assuaged when he imagines a scary day. His "what ifs" of fear are replaced with "what ifs" of love until he can fall back to sleep.

Reviews not available.

Tunnell, Michael O. *Halloween Pie.* Lothrop, Lee & Shepard, 1999. Illustrator: Kevin O'Malley. Grades K-1

A witch makes pie on Halloween, sets it in the window to cool, and chants a spell over it to protect it from being eaten by others. Either the spell didn't work, or it worked just as she planned, for when she returns, the ghoul, banshee, and other creepies that ate the pie have been transformed into the ingredients that she needs to make a new pie.

BL 09/15/99, SLJ 09/99

Updike, David. *An Autumn Tale.* Pippin Press, 1988. Illustrator: Robert Andrew Parker. Grades 1-3

On the eve of Halloween, a boy named Homer places a jack-o'-lantern on his head. In this condition, he and his dog are invited to a gathering of the neighborhood trees, which, as they explain, gather for every full moon. This is a strange book to say the least.

BL 10/15/88, NYTBR 10/30/88

Vainio, Pirkko. *Don't Be Scared, Scarecrow.* North-South Books, 1994. Illustrated by the author. Grades K-1

First published in Switzerland, this is the story of a scarecrow that is not scary. Feeling like a failure, he leaves his farm and travels. Then he discovers what a good scarecrow he really is.

KR 06/15/94, PW 06/13/94

Van Allsburg, Chris. *The Widow's Broom.* Houghton Mifflin, 1992. Illustrated by the author. Grades 3-6

Widow Minna Shaw causes a commotion when she uses a magical broom left behind by a witch. "It's evil," declare the neighbors, although it is only performing household chores. Faced with a possible "burning at the stake," the widow uses her wits to keep the useful broom.

BL 09/15/92, LT 09/92

Vande Velde, Vivian. *Troll Teacher.* Holiday House, 2000. Illustrator: Mary Jane Auch. Grades K-2

Elizabeth's teacher, Miss Turtledove, is a troll, complete with hairy knuckles, purple skin, and orange eyes. Nobody seems to notice or care because the adults all praise her work. Elizabeth devises a plan that will send the principal off with the troll, but little does she know what substitute is lurking in the hallway.

BL 11/15/00, KR 9/1/500

Washington, Donna. *A Big, Spooky House*. Hyperion, 2000. Illustrator: Jacqueline Rogers. Grades K-3

This is the traditional folktale, "Martin's Coming," illustrated and wonderfully retold. A big, strong man who is traveling comes upon a big, spooky house. He's a BIG man and a STRONG man, and he won't be turned away by some scary cats…or will he?

BL 9/15/00, SLJ 9/00

Watson, Wendy. *Boo! It's Halloween*. Clarion, 1992. Illustrated by the author. Grades 2-5

This story of a family preparing for Halloween night has jokes and riddles interspersed within the format.

BL 09/01/92, SLJ 09/92

Whitcher, Susan. *The Key to the Cupboard*. Farrar, 1997. Illustrator: Andrew Glass. Grades 3-5

A young girl keeps her personal witch, Alice, in a cupboard. When Alice unfolds, the two of them weave a spell and meet a wizard.

BL 9/1/97, SLJ 9/97

White, Linda. *Too Many Pumpkins*. Holiday House, 1996. Illustrator: Megan Lloyd. Grades K-2

If you know this story, you know it is *not* scary, but it does contain jack-o'-lanterns. It typically is used by teachers during fall units and at Halloween. The story is of a woman saddled with pumpkins galore, and, tired of finding creative recipes for them, she uses them to decorate her yard with glowing jack-o'-lanterns.

BL 9/15/96, SLJ 11/96

Williams, Linda. *The Little Old Lady Who Was Not Afraid of Anything*. Crowell, 1986. Illustrator: Megan Lloyd. Grades K-1

This poor woman can't get home without being taunted by everything from a pair of clapping gloves to shaking pants. Since she cannot be scared, she sets the clothing articles to task, and they make the best scarecrow ever.

BL 10/01/86, KR 08/15/86

Willis, Jeanne. *The Monster Bed*. Lothrop, 1987. Illustrator: Susan Varley. Grades K-1

A sweet, dragon monster named Dennis is afraid of humans, but his mother reassures him that humans are not real. A boy wanders into Dennis' cave, and the two frighten one another. Rhyming text and pastel illustrations lend a warm touch to a simple story.

SLJ 06/87, CBRS Spring 1987

Winters, Kay. *The Teeny Tiny Ghost*. HarperCollins, 1997. Illustrator: Lynn Munsinger. Grades K-1

The teeny tiny ghost goes to school and tries to learn the ways of ghosting, but Halloween still seems scary. It is not until his teacher and friends come to visit him that he proves himself ready for the fun of Halloween night.

BL 9/1/97, SLJ 11/97

Winters, Kay. *Whooo's Haunting the Teeny Tiny Ghost?* HarperCollins, 1999. Illustrator: Lynn Munsinger. Grades K-1

The adorable ghosts of Teeny Tiny's class encourage him to be brave and slide down the sliding board. Upon returning to his house, Teeny Tiny finds it disturbed, and he uses his bravery to find the culprit—cousin Brad, who is doing his haunting homework for school.

BL 9/1/99, SLJ 9/99

Winthrop, Elizabeth. *Maggie & the Monster.* Holiday House, 1987. Illustrator: Tomie dePaola. Kindergarten.

Some monsters are NOT scary—just annoying! When Maggie tries to sleep, she is bothered by a clumsy monster that has big feet. This monster, Maggie finds out, is looking for her monster mother, who lives in Maggie's closet.

BL 04/01/87, SLJ 05/87

Winthrop, Elizabeth. *Vasilissa the Beautiful: A Russian Folktale.* 1991. Illustrator: Alexander Koshkin. Grades 2-5

In this elaborately illustrated version of a Baba Yaga story, a beautiful girl uses the help of her doll to escape the clutches of the witch.

BL 05/01/91, SLJ 06/91

Wisniewski, David. *Golem.* Clarion, 1996. Illustrated by the author. Grades 3-6

The original basis for *Frankenstein*, Golem is a giant formed from the earth and mud. He is created by a Rabbi to protect the persecuted Jews of sixteenth-century Prague, and when he has done his job, the monster must return to the earth. This version has extensive text and is intended for older readers.

BL 01/97, SLJ 10/96

Wood, Audrey. *Heckedy Peg.* Harcourt, 1987. Illustrator: Don Wood. Grades K-3

Before going to the market, a mother tells her children, "…don't let a stranger in and don't touch fire." When the witch Heckedy Peg shows the children her gold, they forget all their promises and are turned into different kinds of food before their mother saves them.

BL 9/15/87, KR 8/87

Wood, Douglas. *The Windigo's Return.* Simon & Schuster, 1996. Illustrator: Greg Couch. Grades K-6

The Native American Ojibwe story of a monster's revenge on the humans who outwit and destroy him. Fulfilling his promise to come back to eat them, the monster's ashes are transformed into mosquitoes.

BL 09/15/96, SLJ 11/96

Wooldridge, Connie. *Wicked Jack.* Holiday House, 1995. Illustrator: Will Hillenbrand. Grades 3-5

This is a retelling of the folktale "Wicked John and the Devil." In it, Jack, the meanest old

blacksmith there ever was, pays a kindness to St. Peter and is granted three wishes. Those wishes are enough to save his soul from the devil, but he still wanders the earth, carrying a red-hot coal, the will-o-the-wisp.

BL 11/01/95, SLJ 12/95

Wyllie, Stephen. *Ghost Train: A Spooky Hologram Book*. Dial Books, 1992. Illustrator: Brian Lee. Grades K-2

Three homeless ghouls make an amusement park ride their new haunt. Nine holograms interspersed within illustrations create the illusions of ghosts "appearing" and disappearing.

KR 08/01/92, SLJ 08/92

Yep, Laurence. *The Man Who Tricked a Ghost*. Bridgewater, 1993. Illustrator: Isadore Seltzer. Grades 3-6

A young man named Sung cannot be scared, even by the ghost who is planning to kill him. Sung convinces the ghost to teach him the tricks of the ghost trade and then destroys his opponent with human spit.

BL 06/01/93, SLJ 09/93

Yolen, Jane. *Beneath the Ghost Moon*. Little, Brown, 1994. Illustrator: Laurel Molk. Grades K-2

Told in rhyme, this poem has a similar feel to '*Twas the Night Before Christmas*. It is not scary and shares the story of mice frightened from their home by creepy lizards. The mice strike back to reclaim their territory, and in celebration, they dance under the moon with a new friend.

BL 09/15/94, LT 09/94

Ziefert, Harriet. *Two Little Witches: A Halloween Counting Story*. Candlewick, 1996. Illustrator: Simms Taback. Kindergarten

Beginning with one little witch meeting another little witch, the story counts and then disperses children tiptoeing up to a spooky old house. When a monster opens the door, he scares them all, except for the two little witches.

BL 9/1/96, SLJ 12/96

I-Can-Read Books and Easy Chapter Books

These books are targeted for beginning readers (K-2). They are not scary and can be read aloud to the youngest audiences.

Allen, Laura Jean. *Rollo and Tweedy and the Ghost at Dougal Castle*. HarperCollins, 1992.
Rollo and Tweedy, two tiny but efficient mice, solve small-time crime. When Lord Dougal asks the mice detectives to solve the mystery of the ghost haunting at Dougal Castle, the mice discover something more interesting than ghosts.
BL 6/15/92, CCB-B 9/92

Cushman, Doug. *Aunt Eater's Mystery Halloween*. HarperCollins, 1998. Illustrated by the author.
Aunt Eater solves some of the neighbor's troubles when she finds a missing daddy who has eaten too much candy, bears dressed as headless ghosts, and a missing snake playing a haunted piano.
BL 09/01/98, SLJ 10/98

Dodds, Dayle Ann. *Ghost and Pete*. Random House, 1995. Illustrator: Matt Novak.
A boy discovers a friendly ghost in his attic. The two go trick-or-treating, but Ghost cannot figure out how to interact politely with human adults. As a result, he receives no candy, but Pete shares his lollipop, and Ghost is pleased.
SLJ 3/96, EL 11/95

Goldsmith, Howard. *The Twiddle Twins' Haunted House*. Mondo Publishing, 1997. Illustrator: Jack Kent.
The twins are hippopotamuses, and when they move into a new house, they search high and low for the cause of a tapping noise. Convinced they have a ghost on their hands, they are surprised to find the culprit is a bird.
SLJ 9/97

Greer, Gery and Rob Ruddick. *Billy the Ghost and Me*. Harper Trophy, 1997. Illustrator: Roger Roth.
In the western town where she wants to become deputy, Sarah and her ghostly friend Billy outwit two bank robbers and save the day.
BL 11/1/5/96, SLJ 3/97

Hautzig, Deborah. *Little Witch's Big Night*. Random House, 1984. Illustrator: Marc Brown.

Little witch has been naughty, and as punishment she must stay home alone on Halloween night. She makes the most of her situation, offering trick-or-treaters a ride on her flying broomstick. Two other stories of Little Witch (*Little Witch Goes to School* and *Happy Birthday, Little Witch)* are included in a video.

BL 12/15/84, SLJ 12/84

Koontz, Robin Michael. *Chicago and the Cat: The Halloween Party*. Cobblehill, 1994. Illustrated by the author.

A rabbit and a cat, the odd couple of the animal world, are invited to a Halloween party. They plan a two-part costume, but their plans go awry.

BL 09/15/94, SLJ 09/94

Levitt, Sidney. *The Mighty Movers*. Hyperion, 1994. Illustrated by the author.

Fred and Ted, the moving men of the bear world, advertise that they can move anything. When a ghost needs to be relocated from its regular haunt, it is more of a challenge than the mighty movers expected.

BL 04/01/94, SLJ 08/94

Maitland, Barbara. *The Bookstore Ghost*. Dutton, 1998. Illustrator: Nadine Bernard Westcott.

The Black Cat Bookstore is haunted, or so they say. Mr. Brown's store sells only scary stories, and he has a black cat. When mice begin causing mischief, customers fear a ghost and stay away until the cat devises with a plan.

BL 11/01/98, SLJ 11/98

Marshall, Edward. *Four on the Shore*. Dial, 1985. Illustrator: James Marshall.

Trying to get rid of Willie, Spider's pesky younger brother, friends tell him scary stories to no avail. Of course, Willie knows a thing or two, and in the end, he scares all of them with a REALLY spooky tale.

BL 3/15/85, SLJ 5/85

O'Connor, Jane. *The Teeny Tiny Woman*. Random House, 1986. Illustrator: R. W. Alley.

A teeny tiny woman takes a teeny tiny bone from a graveyard, but that night, the owner, a ghost, wants it back. His teeny tiny voice grows louder and louder until the woman yells, "TAKE IT!" And the ghost does.

BL 12/1/86, SLJ 12/86

Pilkey, Dav. *Dragon's Halloween*. Orchard, 1993. Illustrated by the author.

Dragon makes a jack-o'-lantern, gets a scary Halloween costume, and is frightened by his own growling stomach in these three easy chapters.

BL 09/15/93, SLJ 10/93

Rubel, Nicole. *The Ghost Family Meets Its Match*. Dial, 1992. Illustrated by the author.

Happy for 100 years, this ghost family has scared everyone from their house. When new tenants arrive, they present a challenge, for they have a few tricks of their own.

BL 06/15/92, KR 09/01/92

Ruelle, Karen Gray. *The Monster in Harry's Backyard*. Holiday House, 1999. Illustrated by the author.

Harry's new tent seems like a great birthday present until his mother suggests he use it outside one night. All goes well until his fear of the dark overwhelms him, and he runs inside to escape the nighttime monster.

KR 2/1/99

Rylant, Cynthia. *Henry and Mudge Under the Yellow Moon: The Fourth Book of Their Adventures*. Simon & Schuster, 1987. Illustrator: Sucie Stevenson.

Henry and his big dog Mudge have autumn adventures, including a Halloween scare when Henry's mom tries some storytelling.

BL 12/01/87, SLJ 04/88

Schwartz, Alvin. *Ghosts! Ghostly Tales from Folklore*. HarperCollins, 1991. Illustrator: Victoria Chess.

These are easy, fun stories with silly pictures. Notes on sources are included.
1. The Haunted House: Two children walk through an old, empty house, try to scare one another, and get scared by a green blob of a ghost.
2. Susie: The ghost of a cat is not for sale at the pet shop.

BL 09/15/91, SLJ 09/91

Schwartz, Alvin. *In a Dark, Dark Room and Other Scary Stories*. HarperCollins, 1984. Illustrator: Dirk Zimmer.

These great short stories for beginning readers and storytellers are illustrated with spooky and funny pictures.
1. The Green Ribbon: When Jenny's green ribbon comes off, so does her head.
2. In a Dark, Dark Room: Everything is dark, dark—perfect for the jump tale ending of a ghost to pop out.
3. The Night it Rained: The ghost of a boy is given a ride, and the driver's sweater is found on the grave the next day (Vanishing Hitchhiker).

BL 04/15/84, SLJ 05/84

Sharmat, Marjorie Weinman. *Nate the Great and the Halloween Hunt*. Coward McCann, 1989. Illustrator: Marc Simont. Grades 1-2

When Nate and his dog Sludge try to solve the case of the missing cat, they find themselves scared in a haunted house. Some cases are better left unsolved.

LT 09/89, SLJ 10/98

Smith, Janice Lee. *Wizard and Wart.* HarperCollins, 1995. Illustrator: Paul Meisel.

A wizard named Wizard and his dog Wart open a business to help solve problems. As animals arrive and request transformations, Wizard and Wart create more problems than they fix.

SLJ 07/95, RT 10/95

Smith, Janice Lee. *Wizard and Wart at Sea.* HarperCollins, 1995. Illustrator: Paul Meisel.

The Henry and Mudge of the wizard world, Wizard creates awful spells, and Wart, his dog, eats them.

BL 07/95, HBG Fall 1995

Spirn, Michele Sobel. *A Know-Nothing Halloween.* HarperCollins, 2000. Illustrator: R. W. Alley.

Best friends Boris, Morris, Dorris, and Norris don't know much, but they manage to have fun in three short stories: "Halloween Tricks," "Hiding from Halloween," and "Where is Dorris?"

BL 9/1/00, SLJ 10/1/00

Stamper, Judith Bauer. *Five Creepy Creatures.* Scholastic, 1997. Illustrator: Tim Raglin.

More fun and puns with monsters that need hugs, give tickles, and tell knock-knock jokes. Try "Stop that Coffin" (use a cough drop) for a laugh.

PW 10/6/97

Stamper, Judith Bauer. *Five Funny Frights.* Scholastic, 1993. Illustrator: Tim Raglin.

Silly spooky stories, including the traditional "Bloody Fingers." No one will be scared, but young readers will enjoy the laughs.

Reviews not available.

Stamper, Judith Bauer. *Five Goofy Ghosts.* Scholastic, 1996. Illustrator: Tim Raglin.

This is just what the title says—five silly stories about people who find themselves surprised by ghosts. Two stories are jokes, one is a cumulative tale, and the others are folktale adaptations.

Reviews not available.

Ziefert, Harriet. *Halloween Parade.* Viking, 1992. Illustrator: Lillie James.

Allie gets ready for the school's Halloween parade. The night before, she has trouble sleeping. After the parade, prizes are given, including prizes for prettiest, ugliest, and scariest costumes.

HBG Spring 1993

Transitional Fiction (Grades 2-4)

These books are typically the "thin" chapter books—more difficult than the easy chapter books, but not quite full-length novels. They are usually illustrated, and in some instances, I've included lengthy picture books or hybrid picture/chapter books. With a few noted exceptions, most are appropriate for grades 2-4.

Brennan, Herbie. *Emily and the Werewolf.* Margaret K. McElderry Books, 1993. Illustrator: David Pace. 92pp. Grades 3-6
    Originally published in England, this is a hybrid picture book with extensive text. Emily wants to stop Farmer Osboro from continuing his werewolf ways, so she hypnotizes him. He, in turn, returns a favor by helping Emily's mom at work.
    Reviews not available.

Conford, Ellen. *Diary of a Monster's Son.* Little Brown, 1999. Illustrator: Tom Newsom. 76pp. Grades 2-4
    Bradley has no mother, and his father is a monster. The book is a brief account of Bradley's somewhat uneventful days. The reader must guess what the father looks like since the illustrations keep the monster's head out of view.
    BL 7/99, SLJ 7/99

Creech, Sharon. *Pleasing the Ghost.* Harper Trophy, 1996. Illustrator: Stacey Schuett. 89pp. Grades 3-4
    Dennis is one of those boys that can see ghosts. They don't scare him, and one day, his Uncle Arvey appears. He tells Dennis how to finish three tasks to help Arvey's widow, Aunt Julia. In the process, Dennis realizes he may one day see the ghost of his own dead father.
    BL 9/1/96, SLJ 11/96

Cuyler, Margery. *Weird Wolf.* Holt, 1989. Illustrator: Dirk Zimmer. 72pp. Grades 3-5
    Harry is of werewolf blood, and upon his first transformation, he craves McDonalds' hamburgers. As each full moon brings embarrassing results, he realizes he needs help, and his friend Abby lends a hand.
    BL 12/1/89, LT 3/90

Delton, Judy. *Camp Ghost-Away.* Dell, 1988. Illustrator: Alan Tiegreen. 80pp. Grades 2-4
    The Pee Wee Scouts sell donuts to raise money for a camping trip. When they arrive at the camp, a strange and scary voice scares them during the night.
    BL 06/01/88

Dickens, Charles. *A Christmas Carol*. Creative Education, 1990. Illustrator: Roberto Innocenti. Grade 4 & Up

This book takes the format of a lengthy picture book, with realistic illustrations and large type. The language remains as Dickens wrote it, which may be difficult for younger readers.
Reviews not available.

Fleischman, Sid. *The Midnight Horse*. Greenwillow, 1990. Illustrator: Peter Sis. 84pp. Grades 3-6

The ghost of a magician comes to the aid of an orphan boy named Touch, providing him with a horse that eventually turns the boy's luck around.
BL 08/90, SLJ 09/90

Harvey, Jayne. *Great-Uncle Dracula*. Random House, 1992. Illustrator: Abby Carter. 76pp. Grades 3-5

Transylvania, U.S.A. is anything but Normal Town, as Emily Normal finds out. Not only are the residents vampires and witches but also the school is full of trouble, from the third grade bully to the strange principal.
HBG Spring 1993

Harvey, Jayne. *Great-Uncle Dracula and the Dirty Rat*. Random House, 1993. Illustrator: Abby Carter. 62pp. Grades 3-5

The sequel to *Great-Uncle Dracula* finds the Normal children back in school with vampire teachers and Principal Frank N. Stein. When Elliot Normal's pet rat destroys Emily's schoolwork, it's time to send the rat to obedience school.
HB spring 1993, SLJ 02/94

Hautzig, Deborah. *Walter the Warlock*. Random House, 1996. Illustrator: Sylvie Wickstrom. 69pp. Grades 2-4

The Halloween Ball is coming up, and Walter's father requests that Walter zap a song. Walter would rather write music by hand, and decides he must use his heart, not his spells, to share his inner magic.
Reviews not available.

Hiser, Constance. *Night of the Werepoodle*. Holiday House, 1994. Illustrator: Cynthia Fisher. 122pp. Grades 3-4

Imagine a bite from a dog that leaves you as a werepoodle during the full moon. That is what happened to Jonathan as he tried to escape from the class bully, and now he must find a magic chewbone or be a puppy forever.
BL 6/1/94, SLJ 6/94

Hoffman, Mary. *The Four-Legged Ghosts*. Dial, 1993. Illustrator: Laura Seeley. 90pp. Grades 2-3

Carrie, Alex's sister, is an asthmatic, so it is a surprise on his birthday when his parents present him with Cedric, a tiny mouse. Unfortunately, they don't know that Cedric is magical,

and he summons the ghosts of all the deceased house pets. Visible only to the children, they create more mischief than fear, until the situation is resolved by Cedric's true owner.

BL 09/01/93, SLJ 08/93

Irving, Washington. *The Legend of Sleepy Hollow.* Boyds Mill Press, 1992. Illustrator: Michael Garland. 62pp. Grades 5-6

The writing is that found in the papers of the late Diedrich Knickerbocker, so the language is somewhat advanced. It includes full-page, realistic illustrations, but it is twice the length of a typical picture book.

BL 11/01/92, SLJ 11/92

Kline, Suzy. *Horrible Harry at Halloween.* Viking, 2000. Illustrator: Frank Remkiewicz. 38pp. Grades 2-4

Harry comes to school dressed as a plainclothes detective, just in time to discover who has stolen Mary's costume. All the regulars (Song Lee, Doug, and Miss Mackle) of Room 3B appear in this mystery.

BL 9/15/00, SLJ 9/00

Kraan, Hanna. *Flowers for the Wicked Witch.* Front Street & Lemniscaat, 1998. Illustrator: Annemarie van Haeringen. 123pp. Grades 2-5

Wicked Witch bothers the animals so much, that they stop speaking to her. When she packs to leave the forest, they regret their actions and give her flowers.

BL 9/1/5/97, SLJ 7/97

Kraan, Hanna. *Tales of the Wicked Witch.* Front Street & Lemniscaat, 1995. Illustrator: Annemarie van Haeringen. 107pp. Grades 2-5

The witch, a little grumpy but far from wicked, casts spells on the forest creatures—hare, hedgehog, and owl. Her adventures result in friendships, and they recently have become an animated television series.

BL 1/1/96, SLJ 1/96

Kraan, Hanna. *The Wicked Witch Is At It Again.* Front Street & Lemniscaat, 1997. Illustrator: Annemarie van Haeringen. 110pp. Grades 2-5

The witch continues in her harmless ways as the animals wonder how to stop her naughty behavior.

BL 9/1/5/97, SLJ 7/97

Kwitz, Mary DeBall. *Little Vampire and the Midnight Bear.* 1995. Illustrator: S. D. Schindler. 48 pp. Grades 1-3

Little Vampire wants to learn to fly but is having trouble. When Midnight Bear comes to eat Baby Vampira, Little Vampire saves the night without realizing he has attained flight.

BL 10/1/95, HBG Spring 1996

Landon, Lucinda. *Meg Mackintosh and The Mystery at Camp Creepy*. Little Brown, 1990. Illustrated by the author. 60pp. Grades 3-4

In this solve-it-yourself mystery, the reader is challenged to determine the identity of the ghost of Camp Creepy. Using visual and written clues, each page draws Meg and the reader closer to the answer.

SLJ 9/90, HBG 1/90

Leroe, Ellen. *Ghost Dog*. Hyperion, 1993. Illustrator: Bill Basso. 64pp. Grades 2-4

Artie shows off a valuable baseball card, and it is stolen by a unscrupulous man. His new pet, Ghost Dog, rescues the card by stopping the man and chasing him as he tries to escape.

BL 04/01/93, SLJ 06/93

Park, Barbara. *Junie B. Jones Has a Monster Under Her Bed*. Random House, 1997. Illustrator: Denise Brunkus. 69pp. Grades 2-4

The monster is invisible to the human eye, and while Junie B. sleeps, it supposedly fits her head into its mouth (hence, the drool on the pillow). A great monster-removing technique is included: vacuuming under the bed and dumping the contents of the vacuum bag into the trash compactor.

SLJ 11/97

Pearson, Susan. *The Spooky Sleepover*. Simon & Schuster, 1991. Illustrator: Gioia Fiammenghi. 71pp. Grades 3-4

Ernie's guests are sure they hear a ghost at her sleepover. They tell ghost stories, search the house, and have a feast. Before the night is over, they discover the "ghost" was only a kitten.

HBG Spring 1992, SLJ 3/92

Pellowski, Michael. *Ghost in the Library*. Troll, 1989. Illustrator: Robert Durham. 48pp. Grades 2-4

Melanie thinks Morganville is boring until she meets the ghost of Captain Morgan at the library. Demanding that his picture and book be restored, Morgan creates a commotion, and Melanie reconsiders her initial assessment of the town.

Reviews not available.

Ross, Pat. *M & M and the Halloween Monster*. Viking, 1991. Illustrator: Marylin Hafner. 64pp. Grades 2-4

In four chapters, Mandy and Mimi transform their creative ideas into Halloween costumes and their fears of a "chain-dragging basement monster" into new friendships. At a Halloween party, they see how creative they are.

BL 09/15/91, SLJ 12/91

Stevenson, Drew. *Terror on Cemetery Hill: A Sarah Capshaw Mystery.* Cobblehill, 1996. 90pp. Grades 3-5

If Encyclopedia Brown had dreamed of his perfect match, Sarah Capshaw would have been it. When the Wilsonburg Bank is robbed, Sarah, Frog, and Melvin work on solving the mystery. With some silly dialogue and surprising turns, this is a perfect mystery for younger readers. It's not too scary, but it does briefly involve a cemetery.

BL 9/1/96, SLJ 9/96

Wilde, Oscar. *The Canterville Ghost.* North-South Books, 1996. Illustrator: Lisbeth Zwerger. Grade 4 & Up

The retelling of this classic tale as a sophisticated picture book may be effective as a read-aloud for older students. Wilde's story of an American family unappreciative of their new-found ghost is supported by full-page watercolors.

Reviews not available.

Wright, Betty Ren. *A Ghost in the Family.* Scholastic, 1998. 92pp. Grades 3-4

Chad and Jeannie spend time in Aunt Rosebud's house and confront the evil spirit of a thief who had lived there. Perfect for this age level, the ghostly descriptions are scary without being overwhelming.

BL 06/01/98, HBG Fall 1998

Wright, Betty Ren. *The Ghost of Popcorn Hill.* Holiday House, 1993. Illustrator: Karen Ritz. 81pp. Grades 3-5

There are too many lonely ghosts at Popcorn Hill, so Martin and Peter decide to pair up the spirits of a dog and a man.

BL 02/15/93, SLJ 05/93

Wright, Betty Ren. *The Ghost Witch.* Holiday House, 1993. Illustrator: Ellen Eagle. 103pp. Grades 3-5

Jenny wants the residing ghost witch to move out of her house. She convinces it to move into an abandoned home that will be used as a haunted house amusement.

BL 01/15/94, LT 03/94

Wright, Betty Ren. *Haunted Summer.* Scholastic, 1996. 99pp. Grades 3-5

When a music box begins to play by itself, Abby is worried. Her brother thinks she is silly, but Abby and the baby sitter Hannah set out to the graveyard to bury the box at the site of the owner.

BL 04/96, SLJ 05/96

Novels and Booktalks

In your attempt to elevate the standards of children who love scary stories, you will need to move beyond the popular paperback series and promote the untried, interesting books. In this section, you will find books that deal with the supernatural and all that it entails. Hopefully, you will be proud of the titles you recommend.

Plenty of resources offer tips on how to booktalk. Some titles are annotated in the professional resource section of this book. Joni Brodart's *Booktalk!* series is perhaps the most well known, and I recommend *Tales of Love and Terror* by Hazel Rochman. Basically, you want to present a preview, much like you see at a movie theater, which whets the appetite without revealing the entire story. Some tips from Hazel Rochman include:

- Read the book and mark passages so that you can refer to them easily without losing momentum.

- Edit passages as needed, but do not edit out the author's style or difficult words. Readers need to be exposed to vocabulary in order to decide if it is their reading level.

- Never give the story away; leave your listeners wanting to read on.
- Warn about controversial material (wise for scary stories in any situation), but don't exploit it. (Rochman, 6-27).

Booktalking is one of the most effective ways to get lesser known novels and story collections off the shelf and circulating. You don't need to booktalk R. L. Stine because children will find his books on their own. Push them beyond what they know and challenge them, for the appeal of a good scary story will often outweigh a reluctant reader's resistance.

Booktalks

Avi. *Something Upstairs: A Tale of Ghosts.* Orchard, 1988. 120pp. Grades 5-8
    Summary: When Kenny moves into a historical house in Providence, he meets the ghost of a slave murdered in 1800. The ghost transports Kenny back in time to solve, and possibly stop, the murder.
    KR 08/01/88, SLJ 10/88

"Those who cannot remember the past are condemned to relive it." – Santayana

It's night. You're trying to sleep in your bedroom. Your family has just moved into a new house. But it's not a new *new* house; it's a new *old* house—200 years old, with the worn wood and musty smells to prove it. Night sounds, perhaps a bat, maybe a mouse, wake you. The room feels hot, and you get up, using your flashlight to guide you to the

sound. What you see is a ghost of a boy, who emerges from the floor. He wears no shoes, and his clothing is frayed; yet on his back, you can make out a large stain. It is blood. The boy is searching for something, feeling the walls, and when he turns around, your eyes lock. And then, just like that, he disappears with his mystery. Your mind races as you wonder who he is or who he was. How many people lived in this house before you? What was that boy looking for? Why was there blood on his back? Was that a dream or a ghost? Do you believe in ghosts? Of course you do because the next night he is back with his story. His name is Caleb, and he was a slave, but he was murdered one night in the very same room where you sleep. He explains: "A ghost is but a memory of what once was." Who's memory, you question? What could he mean? As the visits continue, you realize memories are powerful—so powerful that you agree to become part of Caleb's memory in order to help him stop his murder. But in someone else's mind there are memories just as strong, and as you travel back in time, you confront the killer. The two memories become entangled, and their power is the power of life over death. Not only do their ghosts haunt you but you also become a spirit in their world, using their memories to lead you through Caleb's death or escape. The last thing you remember is a pistol in your hand, a shot firing, and sudden blackness. You awaken in your bed with your parents downstairs. It was not a dream, but you wonder who was killed? Did you make history or relive it? Find out in this exciting story that keeps the reader riveted to every page.

Conrad, Pam. *Stonewords: A Ghost Story.* Harper & Row, 1990. 130pp. Grades 4-7

Summary: A young girl discovers her best friend is a ghost, and must decide whether to change the events of her death.

BL 3/1/90, SLJ 5/90

Imagine that you are a girl named Louise, motherless and growing up in your grandparents' house. Your best friend is a ghost. She is as real to you as the dolls you play with, but she is unseen by everyone else, except your dog. Some days she is pleasant and kind, and others days Zoe Louise is plain rotten. She comes and goes as she pleases, and you have no idea she is a ghost…until one day. Now imagine that within the blink of an eye, simply by walking through a door, you become a ghost in Zoe Louise's world. Invisible, intangible, and undetected by everyone but Zoe Louise, you walk through her house, and you see how she grew up. You stand in a room that existed 100 years ago, and you see the birthday decorations for your best friend. Then, alarmingly, in a sudden flash, you see how she died tragically on her eleventh birthday. She is your best friend, and if you could change the hands of time, you could stop her death. Would you, even if it meant endangering your life or your friendship?

Coville, Bruce. *The Monster's Ring*. Pantheon, 1982. Illustrator: Katherine Coville. 87pp. Grades 3-6

Summary: Trying to escape the torment of bullies, Russell uses the magic powers from a ring to transform himself into a monster.

BL 12/01/82, SLJ 02/83

> "Powers Dark and Powers Bright,
> I call you now, as is my right.
> Unleash the magic of this ring
> And change me to a monstrous thing."

Did you ever have one of those days…years? You know the kind—you're in a new class, and the bully has picked you to be his favorite target for torture. You wish that just once you could get even, or maybe *more* than even. You'd like to cause a little damage to Muscle-head. Well, if you've ever felt that way, then you know how it's been going for Russell Crannaker, a fifth-grade boy with a fondness for monsters and an uncanny knack for annoying the class bully, Eddie. One afternoon, in an attempt to escape his daily torture, Russell dodges into Elives' Magic Shop, and there the ancient, curious owner presents to him a magical ring. The ring is perfect; how did Mr. Elives know? It has specific instructions that allow Russell to turn into a werewolf, and then return to human form. Perfect for Halloween. Perfect for revenge. There is only one problem: Like most boys, as Russell gains power, he forgets the rules, and these rules deal with magic. What will it be—monster or man? Find out in *The Monster's Ring*.

DeFelice, Cynthia. *The Ghost of Fossil Glen*. Farrar, 1998. 167pp. Grades 5-7

Allie is a sixth-grade girl with an active imagination and a love of fossils. During a fossil search, she is saved from a deadly fall by the ghostly voice of a girl who Allie later discovers was murdered. A mysterious diary and ghostly visions help solve the mystery of the murder while preventing a forest glen from becoming a housing development.

BL 03/15/98, KR 02/01/98

The headlines read,

RESCUE WORKERS SEARCH FOSSIL GLEN FOR MISSING GIRL

The search for Lucy Stiles continues. Village and state police are asking for the public's help in locating an eleven-year-old girl who was last seen by her mother at about 5:30 Wednesday night….

That was four years ago when Allie was in second grade. Now, out on a fossil hunt, Allie wanders down the wrong side of a cliff and nearly falls to her death before a strange voice guides her to safety. With intrigue and confusion, Allie wonders whose voice it is,

but her parents and friends only believe she has an active imagination. Things become stranger when her diary begins to submit written entries to itself, beginning with the mysterious message, "I am L." In desperation, she and a friend, Dub, research the events leading to Lucy Stiles' death while at the same time, Allie finds Lucy's original diary. Within the pages are the events leading up to Lucy's death, which Allie discovers was no accident. A man is responsible for her murder, and Allie owes it to the restless spirit of Lucy to identify him. When the man discovers Allie's meddling, he wastes no time trapping her in the same fossil glen where Lucy met her death. Will he kill Allie in the same way that he killed Lucy, or will the ghost of fossil glen once again offer help? Find out in this book that gives new meaning to the term, "cliff hanger."

Patneaude, David. *Haunting at Home Plate.* Albert Whitman, 2000. 181pp. Grades 5-8
Summary: The ghost of a boy killed in an accident haunts a baseball field, helping Nelson's struggling team win the championship.
BL 9/1/00, SLJ 9/00

Legend has it that Andy Kirk was an ordinary boy who loved baseball. He lived in Rivermist 50 years ago, and when he wasn't playing ball, he perched on a tree limb beyond the field and watched his brother's team play. One day, during a game, he fell 20 feet. It was a terrible accident, and he died on the spot. The game ended, and the field was closed. Parents and friends mourned, and somebody hacked the lowest cedar limbs with a chain saw. The field became known as Phantom Limb Park, and nobody used it for years. Why would they, as it had too many memories, and, they say, it was haunted by Andy Kirk's ghost. Now here we are, our disjointed baseball team, a bunch of stragglers, trying to make it into the playoffs. We don't even have a coach, and our practice field is, you guessed it: Phantom Limb Park. But those stories about Andy haunting the place, they're just stories, right? I mean, leaving messages scratched at home plate is somebody's idea of a joke. Right?

Pullman, Phillip. *Clockwork: or All Wound Up.* Scholastic (Arthur A. Levine), 1998. Illustrator: Leonid Gore. 112pp. Grade 4 & Up
Summary: When a boy makes a deal with a clockmaker, a deadly piece of clockwork comes to life.
BL 09/15/98, HBG Fall 1998

He was an apprentice to a master clockmaker, and his "graduation" day was approaching. In order to become a master, his final exam was not a test, but a masterpiece—a display, a figurine. Assigned to make a cuckoo for the town's great clock, he did nothing. Absolutely nothing. And he told no one, not even his master teacher. On the evening before the unveiling, sitting in a tavern in a gloomy state, he listened to a story

told by the town writer, Fritz. Fritz's latest masterpiece was unfinished, but the story was so creepy that it silenced the grown men around him. The boy visualized the evil doctor, the dead hunter, and the prince. As Fritz spoke, the boy could hear the heart made from clockwork. As Fritz wound up his narrative, the men, frozen, watched as the doctor walks through the tavern door. Yes, it was the same doctor from the story, and he had a surprise for the boy. Oh, that foolish boy. He accepted a gift, and by chance, it was a figurine, for the clock—a metallic knight named Sir Ironsoul. It was beautiful, complete with sword, armor, and magic. But the magic was deadly, and Sir Ironsoul struck more than chimes with his weapon.

Russell, Barbara T. *Blue Lightning*. Viking, 1997. 122pp. Grades 3-6

Summary: The ghost of a boy enters the body of Calvin, a 12-year-old who has been struck by lightning.

BL 02/15/97, HB Spring 1997, LT11/97

Calvin is a 12-year-old boy who loves baseball, and he's just found out that he has made the summer All-Star team. It's a muggy, record-hot day, and perhaps Calvin is distracted because of his excitement; he never notices the lightning in the sky. He picks up his aluminum bat, takes a swing, and CRACK! He is struck by lightning and nearly dies. In the hospital, wavering between life and death, he sees himself on the table, and he sees other spirits. His father, who has been gone since Calvin was a toddler, is there in specter form. Then a boy appears, strangely smirking in Calvin's direction. When Calvin returns home, the hostile boy reappears, only this time from *within* Calvin. He is a ghost named Rory, who hitchhiked in Calvin's body to come back to earth. This spirit-boy is furious about his accidental death, and he later becomes filled with malevolence when he learns of Calvin's chance to pitch in the All-Star league. He begins to haunt Calvin, and his ghostly actions become dangerous. After Rory sets fire to Calvin's home, Calvin must decide how to help Rory resolve his conflict, or he may not live to see his All-Star game.

Sleator, William. *The Beasties*. Dutton, 1997. 198pp. Grades 5-8

Summary: Doug and his sister Colette encounter an underground tribe of creatures that use amputated human parts to replenish their bodies. By enlisting the help of the two children, the tribe changes Doug's feelings, and his empathy saves the colony from loggers destroying the forest.

BL 10/1/97, BR 5/1/98

So, you're going to move with your family to the woods because your father is a botanist. He will be studying fungi for a few months while you and your younger sister, Colette, will be expected to find something meaningful to do. When you tell your friend about this, he gives you a strict and severe warning, so odd that it chills you. "Stay away

from old houses," he says. And not only old houses, he warns, but the woods behind old houses and the logging sites about the woods. And, your friend warns, beware of the beasties. Beasties, you think, what are beasties? But your friend does not explain. When you arrive at the new location, guess what kind of house your parents have chosen? That's right; it's an old house. And guess what your sister finds on the first day? Presents. Presents that lead the two of you out of the house and into the woods. The woods where they are waiting. The beasties. Creatures, created from patched amputated arms and legs, sewn crudely with mismatched human eyes and noses. Surely, they are the most horrific living beings you could have imagined, and the beasties know where you are. They have sent for you; they want to talk. And you now understand you friend's warnings. There is no escape; they have you in their underground home, and they want you.

Vande Velde, Vivian. *Ghost of a Hanged Man.* Marshall Cavendish, 1998. 95pp. Grades 5-7
Summary: An outlaw's very-real ghost returns from the grave one year after his hanging. True to his threat, he kills the people involved in his death and can only be stopped if buried.
BL 11/15/98, SLJ 10/98

In the summer of 1877, the outlaw Jake Barnette was sentenced to die. Before he was hung, he vowed that his spirit would seek revenge upon all who had been part of his conviction, including Ben, Annabelle, and their father, Sheriff Springer. A year after his burial, heavy rains flood the town, and the coffins in the cemetery start coming up. With that, Jake's remains and his evil spirit are released, and sure enough, the deaths begin. First Mr. Chetwin, the foreman in the jury, then Judge Wade. There is little chance for the Springers to escape the same fate. A gypsy girl, Zandra, reads Ben and Annabelle's cards, and sees danger in their future—but also a star, the sign of hope. "Remember the star," she says, adding, "Bury him, as soon as you can." But, it is not soon enough. Jake appears, at their window, and his next victim, Emmett Sanders, falls. Will hope be enough? Who will help stop Jake? Find out in this thriller.

Wright, Betty Ren. *The Dollhouse Murders.* Holiday House, 1983. Reissued in 1996, Scholastic. 149pp. Grades 5-7
Summary: When a girl visits her aunt's house, she sees a dollhouse that magically reenacts the murder that killed her great-grandparents.
BL 10/01/83, PW 09/09/83

"The grandmother doll, in its blue silk dress, had been moving in the parlor the night before, or it had been moved by hands no one could see."
Amy is spending some time with her Aunt Clare, a woman troubled by her past. As Clare attempts to clean out and sell the family's old house, she finds herself troubled by Amy's

interest in a dollhouse. Amy innocently plays with the dolls, but each time Clare looks into the toy house, she sees the doll figures positioned as if they were reenacting a murder. Amy is shocked to discover the true story of the death of her great-grandparents although she was aware something strange had happened to cause their deaths. The dolls continue to reenact the murder until Clare explains the story that happened 50 years ago. The terror of the situation becomes serious, and Amy realizes that she must take action. Who was the murderer? She must find out. This is a suspenseful mystery with a perfect touch of fear.

Adler, C. S. *Ghost Brother*. Clarion, 1990. 150pp. Grades 4-7

Wally's older brother has recently died, and although Jon-o's spirit helps to guide Wally in his attempt to skateboard, Wally must learn to live without him. His mother and aunt don't make life easier, but in time Wally realizes his own strengths and talents.

BL 05/15/90, SLJ 05/90

Anderson, Margaret J. *The Ghost Inside the Monitor*. Random House, 1990. 119pp. Grades 5-7

When her father opens a computer store, Sarah uses a computer that communicates with the ghost of a girl who has lost her "home." Sarah must transport the ghost back to her original house for with each message the ghost pulls Sarah deeper into her own time.

KR 7/15/90, SLJ 10/90

Bauer, Marion Dane. *A Taste of Smoke*. Clarion, 1993. 106pp. Grades 3-5

While camping with her older sister, Caitlin discovers the ghost of a boy killed in a fire years ago. She must help the boy, Frank, leave his earthly life behind, and while doing so, come to terms with her own life.

BL 10/15/93, SLJ 12/93

Bial, Raymond. *The Ghost of Honeymoon Creek*. Face to Face Books, 1997. Illustrator: Anna Bial. 169pp. Grades 5-8

This story continues the adventures of Hank and Clifford, the teenagers in the story collection, *The Fresh Grave*. In this novel, they uncover a ghost who holds a secret that spells murder. A plan is created to expose the truth and set the town at peace again.

Reviews not available.

Brittain, Bill. *The Ghost from Beneath the Sea*. HarperCollins, 1992. Illustrator: Michele Chessare. 129pp. Grades 3-5

The historic Parnell House is about to be turned into a museum, much to three young friends' dismay. Tommy, Books and Harry team with ghosts Horace, Essie, and Ellsworth Parnell to solve the mystery of a crooked poker game, thus determining the true owner of the Parnell House.

BL 12/1/92, LT 5/93

Byars, Betsy. *McMummy.* Viking, 1993. 150pp. Grades 4-6

Is a mummy pod growing in Professor Orloff's greenhouse? Mozie must find out. With his friends, Batty and Valvoline, he uncovers the problem and learns to accept his father's death. While not terribly scary or mummified, this is an enjoyable read.

LT 03/94, HB Spring 1994

Carris, Joan. *Aunt Morbelia and the Screaming Skulls.* Little, Brown, 1990. Illustrator: Doug Cushman. 134pp. Grades 3-5

Aunt Morbelia loves to tell spooky stories—the kind of stories that give Todd nightmares. One night, he and his friend, Jeff, go on a secret haunting, break a window, and start a cat yowling. That stunt spooks everyone and leads to punishment for the boys.

KR 10/01/90, SLJ 08/90

Carris, Joan. *A Ghost of a Chance.* Little, Brown, 1992. Illustrator: Paul Henry. 144pp. Grades 5-7

While on vacation in North Carolina, Punch and Tom plan to hunt for Blackbeard's treasure. Punch's dad puts a crimp in their plans when he arranges for Skeeter Grace, a local boy, to give the "Yankees" a tour. There is only one small part in which the boys encounter a "ghost," who is not a ghost at all, but a landowner trying to give a good scare.

BL 03/15/92, SLJ 04/92

Casanova, Mary. *Curse of a Winter Moon.* Hyperion, 2000. 137pp. Grades 4-8

Although this book is slotted for historical fiction, it makes use of the hysteria of the loup garou, or werewolf, feared in France in the 1500s. The story focuses on Marius and his brother John-Pierre, who is cursed with a December 24th birthday, which in that day was thought to be a sign of the devil's work. The boys fight to survive against church power, corruption, and illiteracy in this action-packed, informative account of sixteenth-century Europe

BL 10/15, SLJ 10/00

Climo, Shirley. *T. J.'s Ghost.* Thomas Crowell, 1989. 151pp. Grades 5-7

While staying at her relatives' house, T. J. is called by a ghost hidden in fog. She discovers a boy, long deceased but obsessed with finding a ring. This quest leads T. J. on an adventure to discover The Coya, a ship that sank 120 years earlier.

BL 6/1/89, KR 3/15/89

Cooper, Susan. *The Boggart.* Margaret K. McElderry Books, 1993. 196pp. Grades 4-8

Accidentally transported to Canada from its old castle in Scotland, the Boggart unintentionally creates danger for a family. The children, Emily and Jessup, finally discover a way, using computer technology and a little luck, to send the Boggart home.

BL 01/15/93, HB Spring 1993

Cooper, Susan. *The Boggart and the Monster.* Margaret K. McElderry Books, 1997. 185pp. Grades 4-8

A companion to *The Boggart*, this story is set in Loch Ness, where the Boggart discovers his long-lost cousin, Nessie, the famous monster. Nessie has forgotten the joys of shape shifting and mischief-making, so it is up to the Boggart to convince his "Cuz" to get out of the lake and back into a castle before scientists discover him.

 BL 03/01/97, HB 05/97

Corbett, Scott. *Witch Hunt.* The Atlantic Monthly Press, 1985. 135pp. Grades 5-8

 When a man is murdered, local witches are suspected of foul play. Lester and Wally, teenage detectives, help identify the murderer and set things straight. This is a suspenseful story, and some of it entails witch gatherings and rituals.

 SLJ 11/85

Coville, Bruce. *The Ghost in the Big Brass Bed.* Bantam Skylark, 1991. 184pp. Grades 4-6

 Nina Tanleven and Chris are thrilled to work in an antique shop where they encounter Phoebe, an old woman whose house is haunted. The ghosts who appear help Nina reveal the mystery behind a missing work of art, and they prevent Phoebe from selling her house and fortune.

 SLJ 01/92

Coville, Bruce. *The Ghost in the Third Row.* Bantam Skylark, 1987. 134pp. Grades 4-6

 Part of the Nina Tanleven ghost series, this story involves the appearance of a deceased famous actress, whose spirit is named The Woman in White. When Nina gets a part in an upcoming play, the ghost upsets rehearsals and props. Nina and her friend Chris discover who is really behind the hauntings.

 BL 09/15/87

Coville, Bruce. *The Ghost Wore Gray.* Bantam Skylark, 1988. Grades 4-6

 Nina and her boy-crazy friend Chris discover the secret that a Confederate ghost is keeping when they travel to a historical bed and breakfast. Slavery and the Underground Railroad all play a part in this mystery.

 BL 9/1/5/88, SLJ 9/88

Coville, Bruce. *Goblins in the Castle.* Minstrel, 1992. Illustrated by Katherine Coville. 164pp. Grades 3-6

 In this funny and not-too-scary story, a boy named William releases goblins and must stop the war between them and the humans. His friends Igor and Herky (a cute goblin) help.

 BL 02/01/93

Cullen, Lynn. *The Backyard Ghost.* Clarion, 1993. 149pp. Grades 4-6

 Eleanor is having a hard time making friends, and the situation becomes worse when a nerdy classmate discovers a ghost in Eleanor's backyard. The students all want to see the Civil War boy soldier, but when they arrive for a viewing, the ghost hides, making things worse for

Eleanor. She eventually helps the ghost and herself in the process, and discovers the true meaning of friendship.
BL 06/01/93, SLJ 05/93

Curry, Jane Louise. *Moon Window*. Margaret K. McElderry Books, 1996. 170pp. Grades 4-6
JoEllen is transported through time when she steps through the window in her cousin's old house. Part fantasy, part mystery, and part haunted house, this story is not scary, but it is suspenseful and enjoyable.
HBG Spring 1997, SLJ 12/96

Cuyler, Margery. *The Battlefield Ghost*. Scholastic, 1999. 103pp. Grades 3-6
When fourth grader John and his sister Lisa move into an old house in Princeton, New Jersey, they find it haunted by the ghost of a Hessian soldier from the Revolutionary War and try to reunite him with the ghost of his beloved horse.
BL 11/15/99, SLJ 12/99

Dahl, Roald. *The Witches*. Farrar, 1983. Illustrator: Quentin Blake. 221pp. Grades 4-6 🔊
Children must avoid the gathering of witches to avoid being turned into mice. While on vacation, they spot witches, identified by their gloves, wigs, and blue spit. Amusing, somewhat scary, and twisted in the typical Dahl style.
HB 04/84, SLJ 01/84

Deem, James. *The Very Real Ghost Book of Christina Rose*. Houghton Mifflin, 1996. 158pp. Grades 5-7
In this story, we read *Christina Rose's Book of Ghosts*, which is an account of her life and ghostly sightings since her mother died in a plane crash. We meet her father, a skeptic on the subject of ghosts, her twin brother, and the family's new Californian neighbors as Christina shares the investigations of her ghost-hunting expeditions. Not terribly scary, but interspersed with some short ghost stories, this story is told in a personal, conversational style.
BL 05/01/96, SLJ 05/96

Dexter, Catherine. *A Is for Apple, W Is for Witch*. 1996. Grades 4-6
Ten-year-old Apple can't wait to practice witchcraft, so when Barnaby teases her, she finds the perfect opportunity to cast a spell. Unfortunately, the small spell leads to big problems.
BL 09/05/96, KR 05/01/96

Dunlop, Eileen. *The Ghost by the Sea*. Holiday House, 1996. 150pp. Grades 5-7
After her brother Tom is seriously injured, Robin stays with her grandmother in a house haunted by Milly, a girl who drowned years ago. While investigating the death, Robin and her cousin are bothered by the spirit, but they eventually learn of the incidents connecting the ghost and Tom.
BL 1/1/97, SLJ 3/97

Dunlop, Eileen. *The House on the Hill.* Oxford University Press, 1987. 147pp. Grades 6-8

A mystery arises when two cousins, Philip and Susan, investigate the eerie glow that emerges each night from behind a closed door. They reveal not only spooky happenings but also family secrets that have kept Aunt Jane bitter for many years.

BL 10/15/87, KR 10/01/87

Farmer, Penelope. *Thicker Than Water.* Candlewick, 1989. 205pp. Grades 5-6

The ghost of a boy killed in a mining accident haunts an orphan named Will. The two share the bond of being orphans, but the ghost torments the living, demanding a proper burial.

GP 05/90, JB 02/90

Fleischman, Sid. *The 13th Floor: A Ghost Story.* Greenwillow, 1995. Illustrator: Peter Sis. 134pp. Grades 3-6 🔊

When his older sister disappears, 12-year-old Buddy Stebbins follows her back in time and finds himself aboard a 17th-century pirate ship captained by a distant relative. Independently, Buddy and Liz find their way back to 1692 Massachusetts and help a 10-year-old girl accused of witchcraft. This story is fun and action-packed, with rogues and rascals typical of Fleischman's work.

BL 10/01/95, SLJ 10/95

Fleischman, Sid. *The Ghost in the Noonday Sun.* Greenwillow, 1965. Reissued in 1991, Scholastic. Illustrator: Peter Sis. 131pp. Grades 4-6 🔊

Because he was born at the stroke of midnight, it is believed that Oliver Finch can see ghosts. Pirates bring the boy to an island where legend states that the ghost of Gentleman Jack can be seen guarding his treasure. It will be Oliver's duty to find the ghost and bring forth the treasure before the scoundrels have a chance to change the conditions.

Reviews not available.

Griffith, Helen V. *Cougar.* Greenwillow, 1999. 106pp. Grades 3-5

Since Nickel moved in with Mom and Pop, he has seen the ghost of his father's large, black horse. When bullies from the school attempt to cause harm, the spirit of the horse comes to Nickel in the form of a racy black bicycle with a will of its own.

BL 4/1/99, SLJ 5/99

Hahn, Mary Downing. *The Doll in the Garden: A Ghost Story.* Clarion, 1989. 128pp. Grades 3-6

After the death of her father, Ashley and her mother move to a new town to start over. Ashley makes friends with Kristi, and together they unearth an antique doll buried in the crotchety landlady's forbidden garden. They discover that they can enter a ghostly turn-of-the-century world, and there they resolve a conflict long neglected by Miss Cooper, the owner of the house and garden.

BL 03/15/89, SLJ 05/89

Hahn, Mary Downing. *Time for Andrew: A Ghost Story.* Clarion, 1994. 165pp. Grades 5-7
When he goes to spend the summer with his great-aunt in the family's old house, 11-year-old Drew is transported 80 years into the past to trade places with his great-great-uncle Andrew who is dying of diphtheria. They agree to stay in warped time until Drew wins a game of marbles, but there is fear that Andrew will not want to give up his comfortable life.
BL 04/01/94, SLJ 05/94

Hahn, Mary Downing. *The Time of the Witch.* Avon, 1982. 171pp. Grades 5-8
Laura is desperate for her parents to get back together. When she meets the believed witch in the hills near her aunt's home, she accepts help, and the spell cast has terrifying results. Only through the help of another witch can Laura stop her brother's near-fatal illness. In the process, she learns to accept life for what it is.
BL 10/15/82, SLJ 11/82

Hahn, Mary Downing. *Wait Till Helen Comes: A Ghost Story.* Clarion, 1986.184pp. Grades 5-7
A new family is formed when Molly and Michael's mother remarries. Their stepsister, Heather, is difficult and annoying, and she seems to be drawn to an old graveyard beside a pond. One of the graves belongs to a girl named Helen, who tries to lure Heather to her death. Molly must fight Helen and put the family ghosts to rest, literally and figuratively.
BL 09/01/86, SLJ 10/86

Hearne, Betsy. *Eli's Ghost.* Macmillan, 1987. Illustrator: Ronald Himler. 103pp. Grades 3-5
While searching for his mother, Eli nearly drowns in a whirlpool, but his ghost escapes his body. The ghost enjoys Eli's life and causes much more mischief than Eli ever did. Eli enjoys being with his "swamp witch" mother, and so the two remain there.
BL 04/01/87, SLJ 04/87

Hughes, Dean. *Nutty's Ghost.* Atheneum, 1993. 136pp. Grades 5-7
Nutty knows it is a crummy movie, but he has been offered the starring role, so of course, he wants to take it…that is, until a ghost decides to stop production. In typical Nutty fashion, this story is more amusing than scary.
HBG Fall 1993

Jensen, Dorthea. *The Riddle of Penncroft Farm.* Harcourt, 1989. 180pp. Grades 5-8
Part of the *Great Episodes* series of historical fiction, this is not a scary book although it employs a storytelling ghost of a teenage boy to relate fascinating events from the American Revolution. Lars, a sixth-grade boy new to Pennsylvania, becomes the captive audience of Geordie, the spirit who helps him not only with history homework but also with the secret to uncovering his grandmother's will. Maps and a glossary are included.
BL 10/1/89, SLJ 10/89

Kamida, Vicki. *Night Mare.* Random House, 1997. 192pp. Grades 5-8
    Janet would love to own a horse, but her family cannot afford one. Her dreams come true one night as a wild mare approaches her window and leads her on a ride that haunts her soul. In the arroyo, Janet meets the owners, not realizing until much later that she has encountered ghosts. This is not a scary story, but it is satisfying for horse lovers.
    BL 11/1/97, SLJ 11/97

Kehret, Peg. *Horror at the Haunted House.* Pocket Books, 1992. 132pp. Grades 5-8
    While acting in a historical production, Ellen discovers that she is a medium for spirits. The ghost of Lydia Clayton, once a resident of the mansion involved, wants to protect her china, and she uses Ellen to carry out her wish.
    BL 09/01/92, SLJ 09/92

Kimmel, Elizabeth Cody. *In the Stone Circle.* Scholastic Press, 1998. 225pp. Grades 5-8
    While on a summer trip to Wales, Cris discovers a ghost in the castle where she and her father are staying. The story line incorporates Cris' deceased mother, and the ending finds Cris uncovering research that leads both the ghost and her own heart to rest.
    CCB-B 3/98, SLJ 4/98

Lehr, Norma. *The Shimmering Ghost of Riversend.* Lerner, 1991. 168pp. Grades 5-8
    An unsolved murder is revealed when Kathy visits her aunt at Wicklow Manor. With the help of a ghost and some new friends, she discovers family secrets and some historical knowledge of the gold rush. This story is more mysterious than scary.
    BL 10/01/91

Levy, Elizabeth. *The Drowned.* Hyperion, 1995. 190pp. Grades 5-8
    This book is a far cry from the *Something Queer* series for which the author is known. In it, Lily becomes trapped by an insane woman, Mrs. Gurney, whose son died in a drowning accident years earlier. Mrs. Gurney sacrifices a child each year and receives an annual visit from her dead son.
    BL 12/1/95, SLJ 12/95

Mayne, William. *Hob and the Goblins.* DK, 1994. Illustrator: Norman Messenger. 140pp.
    Grades 4-6
    Although this book has the ingredients to produce a spellbinding tale, I didn't find myself completely enthralled. Hob, a good-natured spirit who speaks in the third person, ("Hob hopes this pipe will work again.") protects himself and his "family" of humans from the evil goblins that are planning an attack.
    BL 11/01/94, SLJ 11/94

Mazer, Anne. *The Accidental Witch.* Hyperion, 1995. 123pp. Grades 3-5
    Phoebe's dream of practicing witchcraft comes true when she stumbles unto a secret

witch meeting. Her new powers bewilder her and everyone around her until she learns to keep the actions in control.
BL 11/1/95, HBG Spring 1996

McBratney, Sam. *The Ghastly Gerty Swindle: With the Ghosts of Hungryhouse Lane.* Holt, 1994. Illustrator: Lisa Thiesing. 119pp. Grades 3-5
Thieves steal antiques and the ghosts that go with them before Amy and her friends restore everything to normal. This book is a sequel to *The Ghosts of Hungryhouse Lane.*
BL 11/01/94, HBG Spring 1995

McBratney, Sam. *The Ghosts of Hungryhouse Lane.* Holt, 1988. Illustrator: Lisa Thiesing. 119pp. Grades 3-5
The eccentric ghosts that haunt the house of the Sweet family are in for a surprise when they realize the Sweet children are anything but sweet. A change comes, and the children realize the grief of the ghostly life.
BL 04/01/89, SLJ 05/89

Montes, Marisa. *Something Wicked's in Those Woods.* Harcourt, 2000. 214pp. Grades 6-8
After the death of their parents, Javi and his younger brother Nico move to northern California to live with their Auntie Amparo. Javi uses his psychic power to protect his brother from Hamish, a ghost boy whose body is trapped in a root cellar in the woods. A subplot weaves in Willo, a friend of the family who helps break the language barrier for the Puerto Rican boys.
BL 10/15/00, SLJ 12/00

Mooser, Stephen. *The Hitchhiking Vampire.* Dell, 1989. 119pp. Grades 3-5
Although he's really just a skinny, old prospector, the hitchhiker looks like a vampire, and he makes a bet on Jamie's advice. But if the bet goes sour, will she have to pay with her soul? This is not really scary; it is more about acceptance.
BL 06/01/89, SLJ 04/89

Morpurgo, Michael. *The Ghost of Grania O'Malley.* 1996. 183pp. Grades 5-8
Jessie cannot let Big Hill be turned into a gold mine. It is too precious to her and her Irish heritage. She meets the ghost of Grania O'Malley, who feels the same way. But even with Grania's treasure unearthed, they cannot stop the plans for destruction until Grania enlists some help from dead pirates.
BL 6/1/96, SLJ 7/96

Mullarkey, Lisa Geurdes. *The Witch's Portraits.* Dial, 1998. 183pp. Grades 5-6
For a frightening step up from Roald Dahl's *The Witches,* try this book. Two girls spy on an old woman and discover that she traps people in painted portraits. When they confront her and try to free the pictures, they are caught, and nearly lose their skins to the canvas.
BL 09/15/98, SLJ 10/98

Myers, Anna. *Graveyard Girl.* Walker, 1995. 125pp. Grades 4-7

Eli watches as his mother and sister die from yellow fever and his father flees from the tragedy. He arrives at the local cemetery, to bury his family, but is drawn to Grace, known as Graveyard Girl. When Grace asks him to care for a newly orphaned five-year-old girl, he refuses, knowing how painful giving care can be. The ghost of the girl's mother and Grace convince Eli to change in this touching story.

Reviews not available.

Peck, Richard. *Blossom Culp and the Sleep of Death.* Bantam Doubleday Dell, 1986. 185pp. Grades 5-7

Blossom, well known for her gypsy blood, is caught in a tricky spot when forced to use a Ouija board. She contacts the spirit of an Egyptian princess who commands Blossom and Alexander to find and restore the ancient unsettled remains.

Kliatt 09/87

Phillips, Ann. *A Haunted Year.* Macmillan, 1994. 175pp. Grades 5-8

After spending a lonely time with her aunts, Florence finds a photograph of a deceased cousin, whose spirit she summons to appear. The spirit, George, becomes too familiar with the situation, and when Florence learns of his reputation as a murderer, she must find a way to send him back.

BR 09/94, BL 03/15/94

Regan, Dian. *Monster of the Month Club.* Henry Holt, 1994. Illustrator: Laura Cornell. 143pp. Grades 3-6

Expecting only stuffed animals, Rilla Harmony is overwhelmed with the feeding and care of the real monsters that arrive each month by mail. Because she lives in her mother's bed-and-breakfast, the monsters' habits affect the guests until one guest sets everything right. Follow this story with two other episodes in Rilla's life, *Monsters in the Attic* and *Monsters in Cyberspace.*

BL 01/01/95, SLJ 03/95

Roos, Stephen. *My Favorite Ghost.* Atheneum, 1988. Illustrator: Dee deRosa. 123pp. Grades 4-6

Derek wants to make some money, so he plans a ghostly viewing at the Red Barn Theater. For a small fee, children can see the ghost of Evangeline Coffin. But the plan backfires, and Derek is caught in the act.

BL 04/15/88, SLJ 04/88

Schnur, Steven. *The Shadow Children.* Morrow, 1994. Illustrator: Herbert Tauss. 87pp. Grades 6-8

Although this is a hybrid picture book, the subject matter is sophisticated. Ghosts of children fleeing Nazi Germany haunt the French town of Mont Brulant. When Etienne visits his

grandfather, he sees the children, forcing his elders to relive the horrid past.

Reviews not available.

Seabrooke, Brenda. *The Haunting of Holroyd Hill.* Dutton, 1995. 136pp. Grades 5-8

This is an intriguing story that involves history, mystery, and the supernatural. A ghost of the Civil War haunts Melinda and Kevin's home in Virginia. With their neighbor, Dan, the three friends set out to resolve the ghost's turmoil. In the process, they learn valuable family history and settle a long-standing conflict.

BL 09/01/95, SLJ 04/95

Seabrooke, Brenda. *The Haunting at Stratton Falls.* Dutton, 2000. 151pp. Grades 4-6

When Abby's father is sent to fight in World War II, she moves in with her cousins and aunt. Abby discovers a young ghost, Felicia, who lived during the Civil War. This mourning ghost comes to Abby's aid after an accident in which she would have drowned beneath the ice.

BL 7/1/00, SLJ 8/00

Seabrooke, Brenda. *The Vampire in My Bathtub.* Holiday House, 1999. 150pp. Grades 4-5

Jeff, a 13-year-old, and his family move to an isolated area in West Virginia. While exploring the house, Jeff discovers Eugene, a goofy vampire who hates blood and loves garlic. The vampire requires too much money to care for, so Jeff's sister tries to help. Unfortunately, she alerts Eugene's evil vampire cousin, and the children must find a way to stop the sinister vampire from destroying all of them.

BL 1/1/00, HB 1/1/00

Sleator, William. *Dangerous Wishes.* Dutton, 1995. 179pp. Grades 5-8

Set in Thailand, this story is full of Thai customs and superstitions. A 15-year-old American, Dom, and his family experience bad luck upon their arrival in Bangkok. Dom enlists the help of a native boy, Lek, who has a powerful token that will grant wishes, for a price. The two search for a jade stone that must be returned to a grave, and in the process, Dom finds himself face-to-face with an angry spirit. Suspenseful and cultural, this story would be a sophisticated follow-up for those who enjoyed Benjamin Brittain's *Wish Giver*.

BL 8/95

Snyder, Zilpha Keatly. *The Trespassers.* Delacorte, 1995. 200pp. Grades 5-7

This is not a truly scary story but one that leads two children into danger due to their fascination with a spirit haunting Halcyon House. When Neely and Grub meet Curtis, a boy who has recently moved into the house, they must deal with his unstable personality and his attempt to murder Grub.

BL 06/01/95, LT 09/95

Steiner, Barbara. *Ghost Cave.* Harcourt, 1990. 135pp. Grades 3-5

In a harrowing experience, Marc and his friends explore an unknown cave and find the

grave and artifacts of a Native American boy. His ghost leads the boys to safety, and they return his belongings to the earth.

BL 07/90, SLJ 07/90

Strasser, Todd. *Hey Dad, Get a Life.* Holiday House, 1996. 164pp. Grades 4-6

The father of Sasha and Kelly dies, but his spirit hangs around. After helping with home-work and cleaning, he causes problems until he realizes he is no longer needed.

BL 02/15/97, SLJ 03/97

Tolan, Stephanie S. *Save Halloween!* Morrow, 1993. Illustrated by the author. 176pp. Grades 4-6

When you are the child in a fundamentalist family, Halloween is never easy. Johnna has co-authored a play to help a UNICEF project run by her teacher, which happens to be a Halloween project. Her uncle is visiting, and he wants to banish Halloween celebrations. Caught in the middle, Johnna learns to follow her inner voice.

BL 09/01/93, SLJ 10/93

Tolan, Stephanie S. *Who's There?* Morrow, 1994. 235pp. Grades 5-7

When their parents die, Drew and her brother Evan are sent to live with their aunt and grandfather. A mysterious female ghost has a plan to oust the two children, but the ghost's own secret is revealed, securing the future of the orphaned brother and sister.

BL 09/01/94, BR 09/94

Tunnell, Michael O. *School Spirits.* Holiday House, 1997. 201pp. Grades 5-8

A ghost haunts the new school that Patrick attends. After much searching, Patrick and others uncover the skeletal remains of a boy who was thought to have been kidnapped long ago. With that, the name of the accused kidnapper is cleared, unfortunately 50 years too late.

BL 2/1/5/98, SLJ 3/98

Vande Velde, Vivian. *Never Trust a Dead Man.* Harcourt, 1999. 194pp. Grades 5-9

This book is pure pleasure to read, although it involves a murder, witchcraft, and a dead body resurrected. It is the story of a boy named Selwyn who is wrongly convicted of killing a peer, Farold. When his sentence is carried out, he is condemned to die in the sealed burial cave with the victim. He is found by a witch, Elswyth, and bargains with her to find the real murder-er. This is a funny, suspenseful, and enchanting story.

BL 4/1/99, SLJ 5/99

Vande Velde, Vivian. *There's a Dead Person Following My Sister Around.* Harcourt, 1999. 143pp. Grades 5-8

This funny story uses a realistic approach to capture historical fiction. Even if you don't appreciate the sarcasm in the dialogue, you will certainly appreciate the plot of a sister and brother caught in the trauma of the ghosts of those killed using the Underground Railroad.

BL 9/1/99, SLJ 9/99

VanOosting, James. *Maxie's Ghost.* Farrar, 1987. 118pp. Grades 4-6

Maxwell, or Maxie to his friends, is an orphan living with his sister in the orphanage. On Halloween, his class takes a trip to the orphanage, and through a freak accident, Maxie has an experience that brings him face-to-face with his grandmother's ghost. In the end, Maxie must decide whether to stay on earth with his sister, or go with his grandmother.

KR 10/15/87, PW 10/30/87

Wallace, Barbara Brooks. *Ghosts in the Gallery.* Atheneum, 2000. 136pp. Grades 5-7

In a Victorian mystery, Jenny, an orphan from China, is sent to live with her grandfather in the United States. Upon her arrival, she is forced into a servant's life until she can discover who is out to destroy her and why.

SLJ 7/00, LT 11/00

Windsor, Patricia. *How a Weirdo and a Ghost Can Change Your Entire Life.* Delacorte, 1986. Illustrator: Jacqueline Rogers. 123pp. Grades 3-5

Teddy is the weirdo of the class, and he is bringing Martha the school assignments while she is sick. He also is an expert on the Ouija board, summoning friendly detective ghosts. Martha has a great adventure and learns about making true friends.

KR 09/01/86

Woodruff, Elvira. *The Ghost of Lizard Light.* Knopf, 1999. Illustrator: Elaine Clayton. 176pp. Grades 4-6

Jack and his pet lizard, Ned, become friends with the ghost of Nathaniel, a boy who lived more than 100 years ago. Nathaniel needs Jack to help clear the name of his father—a man who tended the lighthouse, but was accused of negligence after Nathaniel's drowning death.

Reviews not available.

Woodruff, Elvira. *Ghosts Don't Get Goose Bumps.* Holiday House, 1993. Illustrator: Joel Iskowitz. 167pp. Grades 3-5

Imagination runs wild when Angel takes Jenna to see a haunted marble factory. Ghosts, witchcraft, and smuggling all are conjured in the minds of these 11-year-olds, which leads them to embark on a dangerous expedition.

BL 11/15/ 93, SLJ 10/93

Woodruff, Elvira. *The Magnificent Mummy Maker.* Scholastic, 1994. 132pp. Grades 4-6

A talented stepbrother, Jason, has academically overshadowed Andy, but things change during a class trip to a museum. Andy is filled with power after viewing a mummy, and he seems to get everything he wishes for.

BL 01/15/94, LT 03/94

Wright, Betty Ren. *The Ghost Comes Calling.* Scholastic, 1987. 83pp. Grades 3-4

When Chad's father buys a cabin, he buys the ghost that haunts it as well. Chad and

Jeannie must find a way to put the spirit of Tim Tapper to rest.
BL 02/15/94, SLJ 04/94

Wright, Betty Ren. *The Ghost in Room 11*. Holiday House, 1998. Illustrator: Jacqueline Rogers. 112pp. Grades 3-5

Matt is trying to fit into the social life of a new school, but he is not a great student, and he has been caught lying. On a dare, Matt spends a night in his school, but he finds he is not alone when the ghost of a former teacher teaches him a lesson about trying and succeeding.
SLJ 3/98, CCB-B 4/1/98

Wright, Betty Ren. *A Ghost in the Window*. Holiday House, 1987.152pp. Grades 3-6

Meg and Caleb learn that their respective fathers are not all they had hoped they would be. This story about family acceptance of both the living and the dead is not very scary, and there are only slight references to the ghost.
BL 11/15/87, SLJ 10/87

Wright, Betty Ren. *The Ghost of Ernie P.* Holiday House, 1990. 130pp. Grades 4-6

Ernie is an ignorant bully, but Jeff can't stand up to him. When Ernie dies, his ghost comes back to force Jeff to carry out his Top Secret Plan to expose a mentally ill woman as a witch.
BL 12/15/90, HBG 07/90

Wright, Betty Ren. *The Moonlight Man*. Scholastic Press, 2000. 181pp. Grades 5-8

Jenny's new house is inhabited by the spirit of a dead man who is intent on ruining the lives of those who destroyed his chance at love. After confronting neighbors, Jenny realizes she must make peace with the ghost in order for any of them to survive.
BL 2/15/00, LT 5/00

Wright, Betty Ren. *The Scariest Night*. Scholastic, 1991. 166pp. Grades 3-5

Erin is bored by the summer plans forced upon her, and she resents her brother because of it. One night, during a power outage, she ventures to a neighbor's apartment and takes part in a creepy séance, but she realizes real fear has nothing to do with witches or werewolves.
SLJ 10/91

Wright, Betty Ren. *Too Many Secrets*. Scholastic, 1997. 116pp. Grades 3-6

This is another story with Chad and Jeannie, in which the two believe a thief if attempting to rob Chad's summer neighbor. While struggling to solve this mystery, Chad also must confront his father, who has a serious girlfriend. All the secrets come out in the end.
SLJ 8/97, LT 11/97

Reference:

Rochman, H. *Tales of Love and Terror*. Chicago: American Library Association, 1987.

Story Collections

In this section, you will find compilations of stories. Included are both original works and traditional folktale collections. When reading short stories, the range of topics and quality of writing can vary, so I've highlighted those exceptional stories that are the best ones for sharing. Be sure to look at the grade level as some collections include sophisticated stories meant for older students.

Aiken, Joan. *A Foot in the Grave.* Viking, 1989. Illustrator: Jan Pienkowski. 128pp. Grades 6-8
   Most of Joan Aiken's stories are more sophisticated than those selected by my typical readers, but this collection contains shorter stories that are illustrated.
   1. Beelzebub's Baby: Aunt Ada won't listen and insists on taking home the child-spirit of an abandoned baby, with disastrous results.
   GP 5/90, JB 4/90

Alcock, Vivien. *Ghostly Companions: A Feast of Chilling Tales.* Delacorte, 1987. 132pp. Grades 5-8
   These are thoughtful tales, not horrific, but stirring.
   1. The Good-looking Boy: A Greek nymph, Echo, falls in love with a beautiful boy, and he must stop her from ruining his life.
   2. The Whisperer: The ghost of a girl tries to play with her living relatives until they learn how to let her rest in peace.
   BL 6/15/87, BR 11/97

Bang, Molly. *The Goblins Giggle and Other Stories.* Peter Smith, 1988. Illustrated by the author. 57pp. Grades 3-4
   1. Mary Culhane and the Dead Man: A retelling of the story of a girl who must carry around a dead man, and who learns secrets of the dead during the night.
   Reviews not available.

Bauer, Caroline Feller, ed. *Halloween: Stories and Poems.* J. B. Lippincott, 1989. Illustrator: Peter Sis. 76pp. Grades 3-5
   This collection includes stories, poems, and anecdotes.
   1. The Jigsaw Puzzle: As a girl pieces a puzzle together, she sees herself, her room, and a stranger.
   2. The Visitor: A version of *Taily-po* told in rhyme in which a skeleton comes back to claim its stolen ring.
   BL 10/01/89, LT 10/89

Bial, Raymond. *The Fresh Grave and Other Ghostly Stories.* Face to Face Books, 1997. Illustrator: Anna Bial. 145pp. Grades 5-8

This book opens with a narrative by Jarvis Satterly, a resident of Myrtleville, who swears the stories are true. An afterword directs readers to find their own ghost lore at the local library.

1. The Fresh Grave: Grave robbers are thwarted when a teenage boy, Hank, agrees to be buried alive.
2. Haunted Barn: In a barn believed to be haunted, a boy's spirit reveals his skeleton and the story of his murder.

SLJ 12/97

Brown, Roberta Simpson. *Queen of the Cold-Blooded Tales.* August House, 1997. 141pp. Grades 6-8

These disturbing tales include an author's note on why scary stories are important to share.

1. Where Freddy Is: A boy wanders into a witch's yard, and she turns him into a rosebush.
2. Pop-Ups: The heads of two men pop up from the earth under which they are buried.

SLJ 01/98

Brown, Roberta Simpson. *Scared in School.* August House, 1997. 141pp. Grades 6-8

These short stories focus on a school that has been targeted by aliens. The strange (and sometimes extremely short) stories weave together as various children disappear and are murdered while others fight to survive.

SLJ 1/98

Brown, Roberta Simpson. *The Walking Trees and Other Scary Stories.* August House, 1991. 139pp. Grades 6-8

These original stories will chill even the bravest readers.

1. The Walking Trees: Campers try to scare each other with stories of trees that snatch people. In the morning, one camper realizes the truth to the tale.
2. Fish Bait: A boy is doomed to a grisly fate when he catches Old Whiskers.

Bloom Review 12/91, CBW 11/91

Bruchac, Joseph and James Bruchac. *When the Chenoo Howls: Native American Tales of Terror.* Walker, 1998. Illustrator: William S. N. Bock. 136pp. Grades 4-6

This father-son team gives great source notes and has revived some very old tales.

1. Ugly Face: If you're a bad child, your parent may put you outside and tell Ugly Face to take you. If that happens, you may never be seen again.
2. Toad Woman: Told to children to keep them away from the dangerous swamps, this is the story of Toad Woman, who would lure and then drown curious passersby.

BL 8/01/98, BR 01/99

Brunvand, Jan Harold. *The Choking Doberman.* W. W. Norton & Company, 1984. Grade 6 & Up
   Although this title precedes the cut-off date of 1985, it is the standard to use in reference to urban legends. Along with Brunvand's *The Mexican Pet* and *The Vanishing Hitchhiker,* these folktales are meant for upper-level students (sixth grade and above). Be warned that there are some grisly deaths within these pages.
   BL 5/1/84, PW 4/27/84

Carusone, Al. *The Boy With Dinosaur Hands: Nine Tales of the Real and Unreal.* Clarion, 1998. Illustrator: Elaine Clayton. 85pp. Grades 3-6
   Just right for the intermediate grades, these stories will spook, but not scare, most readers.
   1. It Will Grow Back Bigger: When Jeremy picks his scab, it grows larger than he is.
   2. The Funhouse People: At the amusement park, a roller coaster becomes a perpetual ride
   BL 08/98, HBG Fall 1998

Carusone, Al. *Don't Open the Door After the Sun Goes Down: Tales of the Real and Unreal.* Clarion, 1994. Illustrator: Andrew Glass. 83pp. Grades 3-6
   This collection contains nine perfectly scary stories.
   1. Dog Days: After a tragic auto accident, a rude woman is transformed into a dog to replace the one she killed.
   2. Whispered Around Lonesome Campfires: Tom realizes the legend of Kittybunka is true when Alvie disappears in the night.
   HGB Spring 1995, LT 03/95

Cecil, Laura, comp. *Boo! Stories to Make You Jump.* Greenwillow, 1991. Illustrator: Emma C. Clark. 92pp. Grades 3-5
   These easy traditional stories contain not-so-scary illustrations.
   1. The King o' the Cats: The story by Joseph Jacobs.
   2. Scribbling Tess: Told in rhyme, this is the story of Tess, who has become a famous sight scribbling within castle walls.
   BL 01/01/91, LT 03/91

Cohen, Daniel. *Dangerous Ghosts.* Putnam, 1996. 85pp. Grades 5-8
   These ghosts seek to avenge their deaths or cause harm in some way.
   1. Tregagle: Summoned after his death, this ghost of a 17th-century lawyer still haunts parts of Cornwall, England.
   2. The Bandaged Horror: The spirit of a victim of cannibalism comes back to kill his ship mate.
   BL 11/15/96, LT 01/97

Cohen, Daniel. *Ghost in the House.* Cobblehill, 1993. Illustrator: John Paul Caponigro. 88pp. Grades 5-8

> This collection has nine stories of famous haunted houses.
> 1. The Winchester Mystery House: Due to the nature of the Winchester fortune, the family was cursed, and the widow turned slightly mad. Her house contains doors that lead to nowhere, stairs that drop off, and other bizarre features. It is now a tourist attraction in California.
> BL 07/07/93, SLJ 03/94

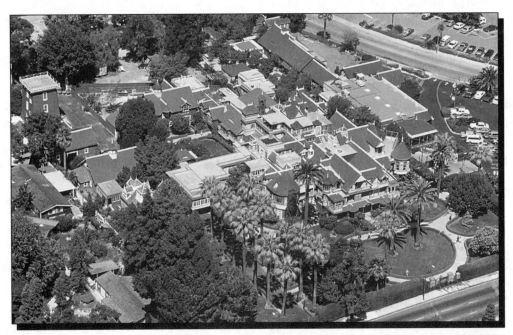

Figure 3.1 The Winchester House, courtesy of The Winchester House, from *Screaming Skulls: 101 of the World's Greatest Ghost Stories* by Daniel Cohen

Cohen, Daniel. *The Ghost of Elvis and Other Celebrity Spirits.* Putnam, 1994. 100pp. Grades 4-6

> This is a compilation of sightings of famous people, now deceased. Included are some of the spirits I want to meet: Edgar Allan Poe at the Poe House in Baltimore, Houdini, and Elvis.
> BL 07/94, SLJ 08/94

Cohen, Daniel. *Ghostly Tales of Love and Revenge.* Putnam, 1992. 104pp. Grades 4-8

> What's better than a scorned woman who just won't give up, even after death?
> 1. Grief: This is the story behind Marion Hooper Adams' monument in Washington, D.C.
> 2. Treacherous Barbara: A man ignores the warning to avoid the beautiful sister of his wife, and he pays dearly in the end.

3. The Lady in Black: Executed as a spy during the Civil War, her ghost haunts Fort Warren, outside Boston.
BL 08/92, SLJ 07/92

Cohen, Daniel. *Ghostly Warnings.* Cobblehill, 1996. Illustrator: David Linn. 64pp. Grades 3-5
These shorter stories deal with the inescapable dealings of fate. Designed to appeal to the younger audiences, this book has large text and illustrations.
1. The Black Velvet Ribbon: One morning, Lady Tyrone appears with a ribbon around her wrist, and from that time, she is able to predict death.
BL 09/15/96, SLJ 10/96

Cohen, Daniel. *Ghosts of the Deep.* Putnam, 1993. 103pp. Grades 4-8
Haunted ships and ghosts of sea travelers are included in these 16 fascinating chapters.
1. Faces in the Water: An actual photograph depicts the faces of two men bobbing in the water. The men had died on an oil tanker and were buried at sea.
2. The Great Eastern: The larger the ship, the greater the profit...or failure. This is the true story of a giant ship cursed with a dead man in its walls.
BL 11/15/93, LT 01/94

Cohen, Daniel. *The Ghosts of War.* Putnam, 1990. 95pp. Grades 5-8
Restless spirits wander, victims of horrid deaths.
1. Rescue My Body: (War of 1812) In a dream, the ghost of a man asks the woman who rejected his love to give him a proper burial.
2. The Cursed Car: (World War I) This is the story of a car owned by the assassinated Archduke of Austria and the deaths that accompanied it.
BL 06/01/90, KR 06/15/90

Cohen, Daniel. *Great Ghosts.* Dutton, 1990. Illustrator: David Linn. 48pp. Grades 4-8
These stories are for the younger audiences of famous ghosts, many in England.
1. The Brown Lady: A shadowy image of a woman, once photographed, haunts the English mansion of Raynham Hall.
BL 10/01/90

Cohen, Daniel. *The Headless Roommate and Other Tales of Terror.* M Evans and Co., 1980. Illustrator: Peggy Brier. 127pp. Grades 5-8
These are the favorite urban legends ("Phantom Hitchhiker," "The Babysitter and the Telephone") along with some of Cohen's original twists.
1. The Man in the Middle: After a lovely night in Manhattan, a woman must ride the subway car to Queens alone. She is unnerved by one of three men staring coldly at her and is told later that the man was a corpse.

Cohen, Daniel. *Phantom Animals.* Putnam, 1991. 111pp. Grades 5-8

Some animals come back as friends, some as foes.

1. The White Rabbit of Crank: Murderers pay with their lives after they spot the ghost of a white rabbit.
2. The Rats of Rhine: After a bishop murders the poor, starving people, rats hunt him down, pursuing him even on an island.

BL 08/91, KR 06/15/91

Cohen, Daniel. *Phone Call From a Ghost: Strange Tales from Modern America.* Dodd, Mead, 1988. 110pp. Grades 5-8

This has been reissued as a paperback, and includes eerie occurrences of spirits contacting Americans.

1. My Hands Are Free from Blood: A ghost of a son tells his family that the reports of his suicide are untrue.
2. Pipe Smoke: A pipe-smoking ghost leads a woman to rescue his widowed wife, who has attempted suicide.
3. The Frenchman's Body: An old hermit exchanges an inscribed lighter for a photograph of another man. Years later, it is discovered the souls have been switched.

BL 6/1/88, SLJ 8/88

Cohen, Daniel. *Railway Ghosts and Highway Horrors.* Dutton, 1991. 109pp. Grades 5-8

This folklore regards "traveling" ghosts.

1. Big Joe: Desolate teen hitchhikers are saved on the highway by the ghost of a truck driver.
2. The Warning Light: To avoid future disaster, the headless ghost of a railroad worker warns his friend to stop the train.
3. Open 24 Hours: In the morning, a man returns to the diner where he had been served the night before, only to find that it had been closed for years.

BL 11/1/5/91, SLJ 10/91

Cohen, Daniel. *Real Ghosts.* Minstrel, 1992. 125pp. Grades 5-8

Reissued from the original 1977 text, these stories are only as real as the reader believes they are. Daniel Cohen is a master at explaining why details and documentation are important, but he makes no promise that these ghosts exist.

1. The Best Ghost Story: A World War I pilot crashes his plane at the exact time he appears in his room to speak with his roommate.
2. The Real Exorcist: Contrary to the movie, which Cohen describes as, "mostly made up," this tells of a boy troubled by spirits in his room, which subside after a visit by a priest.

Reviews not available.

Cohen, Daniel. *Real Vampires.* Cobblehill, 1995. 114pp. Grades 5-8

Included are some facts and some stories about the blood-sucking undead.

1. A vampire in the family: This chapter would be a great follow-up to Cynthia DeFelice's book *The Apprenticeship of Lucas Whittaker.* The family's "vampire" caused deaths during the time when consumption was still a mystery.

HBG Fall 1995, RT 10/96

Cohen, Daniel. *The Restless Dead: Ghostly Tales From Around the World.* Minstrel, 1996. 123pp. Grades 5-7

This book is a reissue of 11 stories written in 1984.

1. The Hooded Chair: A domed leather chair from Holland curses its owners, including Napoleon.
2. The Dust: British naval officers drink with the spirit of a dead woman in Malta.

BL 8/84, SLJ 9/84

Cohen, Daniel. *Screaming Skulls: 101 of the World's Greatest Ghost Stories.* Avon Books, 1996. 205pp. Grades 5-8

This is a compilation of Cohen's favorites, retold in a short form. Most stories are only a page or two, and some include photographs that were not part of previous Cohen publications. Choose from: Famous Ghosts, Haunted Places, Animal Phantoms, Poltergeists, Warnings and Apparitions, Ghostly Phenomena, and Ghostly Legends.

Reviews not available.

Cohen, Daniel. *Werewolves.* Cobblehill, 1996. 117pp. Grades 5-8

For the true fans of this beast. this book contains more advanced, historical writing than other Cohen books.

1. Werewolves of the Internet: You know things are changing when you can go online and chat about sightings and experiences with werewolves.
2. Ten Great Werewolf Films: Included are *An American Werewolf in London* and *Wolf.* These films are rated R, just to give you an idea of the intended audience for the book.

BL 10/01/96, SLJ 03/96

Colby, C. B. *World's Best "True" Ghost Stories.* Illustrated by the author. Sterling Publishing, 1988. 128pp. Grades 3-6

Great for the reluctant reader, these two-page stories are divided into sections that range from "Strange!" to "Tales of Terror."

1. Lord Dufferin's Story: A spirit serves as the deterrent for a man who avoids a deathly elevator ride.
2. The Vanishing Oliver Larch: On Christmas Eve, the last words Oliver's parents heard from above were, "Help! Help! They've got me!"

Reviews not available.

Cole, Joanna, and Stephanie Calmenson, comps. & eds. *The Scary Book*. Morrow Junior Books, 1991. Illustrators: Dirk Zimmer (*Bony-Legs*) and Chris Demarest. 128pp. Grades 2-5

Many of the traditional folktales, such as "Wait Till Martin Comes" and "The Viper is Coming" are included. The section on tricks, games, and other things to do is fun.

1. I Found a Human Finger! Cut a hole in a jewelry gift box so your finger can poke through.
2. How to Draw a Monster, a Werewolf, a Witch, and a Vampire: by Chris Demarest.

BL 08/91, LT 09/91

Coville, Bruce. *Oddly Enough: Stories by Bruce Coville*. Harcourt, 1994. 122pp. Grades 5-6

Nine stories with a note from the author.

1. Duffy's Jacket: Great for reading aloud, this is the story of a monster who stalks a forgetful boy and then reprimands him.
2. With His Head Tucked Underneath His Arm: After a wrongful beheading, Brion emerges from the grave to set things right.

BL 10/01/94, LT 01/95

Coville, Bruce. *Odder Than Ever: Stories by Bruce Coville*. Harcourt, 1999. 146pp. Grades 5-8

These nine stories, reprinted from past collections, are not all scary, but they are certainly odd.

1. The Japanese Mirror: In a land where everything is backwards, Jon must save himself and come to terms with his anger.

BL 05/15/99, PW 05/10/99

Dickinson, Peter. *The Lion Tamer's Daughter and Other Stories*. Delacorte, 1997. 298pp. Grades 5-8

These four well-written stories, three quite lengthy, give a slight chill.

1. The Spring: A boy is drawn to a nearby spring that releases the life of a brother he never knew.
2. Checkers: A boy held hostage is kept alive by the ghost of another boy who had suffered death under the same circumstance.

BL 4/1/97, SLJ 3/97

Don't Read This! And Other Tales of the Unnatural. Illustrator: The Tjong Khing. Front Street Lemniscaat, 1998. 213pp. Grades 5-8

This is an excellent collection of stories by internationally-known authors, including Margaret Mahy and Susan Cooper.

1. Fingers on the Back of the Neck: A boy is haunted after he murders his aunt to receive money to attend private school.
2. The Computer: The ghost of a teenage tennis prodigy urges a boy to compete with his father.
3. Uninvited Guests: After successful hypnotherapy, a boy is relieved of the demons of his mind, but they travel to the mind of the hypnotherapist.

PW 03/01/99

Downer, Deborah L., ed. *Classic American Ghost Stories*. August House, 1990. 214pp. Grades 5-8

This is a well-planned collection of stories from state archives. Librarians of the United States contributed the best of their local folklore, and the result is appealing. Many historical notes are included.

> 1. The Night Call: A doctor makes a house call at the scene of a murder. When he returns the next day with police to investigate, they find nothing but an abandoned shack.

BR 1/91

Durant, Alan, comp. *Vampire and Werewolf Stories*. Kingfisher, 1998. Illustrator: Nick Hardcastle. 220pp. Grades 6-9

This is a sophisticated collection with excellent excerpts from Bram Stoker's *Dracula* and Clemence Housman's *The Werewolf*.

> 1. Getting Dead: A vampire wants to commit suicide to stop his undead life, but he hires a man who turns him into a werewolf.
> 2. Count Dracula: This is a story by Woody Allen about a vampire trapped in a closet.

BL 1/1/99

Emert, Phyllis. *The 25 Scariest Places in the World*. Lowell, 1995. Illustrator: Ted Fuka. 64pp. Grades 3-6

From the Devil's Hole in New York to the Amazon River, there's a spooky story for each location, accompanied by an illustration and map.

SLJ 03/96, KR 07/15/96

Forgey, William W., ed. *Campfire Stories: Things That Go Bump in the Night*. ICS Books Inc., 1985. 📼

Long time camper "Doc" Forgey collects great stories specially designed to spook teenagers around a campfire. Most of them focus on the wilderness and nature, and many of the stories contain a moral. Each story is followed by a concise outline for storytellers to use.

> 1. The Ghost at Sevenoaks: While staying at his friend's house, a man finds that the crazy gardener has beheaded an elderly woman and is plucking her hairs out one by one.
> 2. Cannibalism in the Cars: The author encourages tellers to adapt Mark Twain's flesh-eating story and gives tips on how to do this.

Reviews not available.

Forgey, William W., ed. *Campfire Tales, Volume 2*. ICS Books Inc., 199. Grade 5 & Up

The *Campfire Tales* book, along with Forgey's other two collections, is unique in that it shares an outlined plot for each story for fellow campers who want to try to tell.

Reviews not available.

Forgey, William W., ed. *Campfire Stories, Volume 3: More…Things That Go Bump in the Night.*
ICS Books Inc., 1995. Illustrator: David L. Sanders. 140pp. Grade 5 & Up

This book shares the same style as the *Campfire Tales* and other *Campfire Stories* book.
The original stories hold the flavor of the far-North and include the following:

1. A Knock at the Door: A man stranded in the Canadian wilderness finds the journals of boys that have disappeared after sighting an unknown creature. After he attempts to protect himself, he realizes he has mistakenly shot the pilot that could have led him to safety.
2. The Blemish: This is a fantastic version of the urban folktale in which a girl hatches spiders from a cyst on her face. Gross!

Reviews not available.

Gale, David, ed. *Don't Give Up the Ghost: The Delacorte Book of Original Ghost Stories.*
Delacorte, 1993. 165pp. Grades 5-6

With notes from each author, these 12 stories are of ghosts past, present and future.

1. Variation on a Theme: The Grateful Dead: A dead woman's body is buried by a man, who then becomes an heir to her fortune and is entangled in her pact with the devil.
2. The Face in the Rafters: A father tells his children a "true" ghost story, one that indicates he and their mother will die simultaneously.

BL 08/93, HB Spring 1994

Gibbons, Faye. *Hook Moon Night: Spooky Tales from the Georgia Mountains.* Morrow, 1997.
112pp. Grades 5-8

These eight hair-raising yarns are from the "haints" of Georgia.

1. The Painting: A girl in a painting lures another child to switch places with her.
2. The Burial: When Delvin rushes to bury his mother-in-law, he's tormented with nightmares of being buried with her. He unearths the body to find it in a different position, and disappears soon after.

BL 11/1/97, KR 6/15/97

Gilson, Kristen. *The Baby-Sitter's Nightmare: Tales Too Scary To Be True.* HarperTrophy, 1998.
102pp. Grades 5-7

The best of the urban legends includes "Finger-Lickin' Good" (The Licked Hand) and "The Baby-Sitter's Nightmare" (Phone Call in the House). They are slightly gross, but short and uncomplicated.

CCB-B 11/98, PW 08/31/98

Goode, Diane. *Diane Goode's Book of Scary Stories and Songs.* Dutton, 1994. Illustrated by the author. 64pp. Grades 2-6

These traditional stories and songs include bright pictures.

1. Mr. Miacca: A boy learns that his mother was right after Mr. Miacca pops him into his bag and tries to cook him.

2. 'Tain't So: Old Man Dinkins needs to read his tomb before he believes he is dead.
SLJ 10/94, PW 07/04/94

Gorog, Judith. *In a Creepy, Creepy Place and Other Scary Stories.* HarperCollins, 1996.
Illustrator: Kimberly Bulcken Root. 51pp. Grades 3-4
This collection includes five not-so-scary stories that are good choices for students in second or third grade.
1. Frankenflopper: A doll with a resemblance to a monster gives parents the creeps.
LT 01/97, SLJ 02/01/97

Gorog, Judith. *In a Messy, Messy Room and Other Scary Stories.* Philomel, 1990. Illustrator:
Kimberly Bulcken Root. 23pp. Grades 3-4
Meant to be read aloud or told to an audience, these are five funny, scary stories.
1. Smelly Sneakers: Toad wants to win the contest, but what he uses to make his sneakers smell disintegrates his feet.
BL 06/01/90, KR 05/01/90

Gorog, Judith. *No Swimming in Dark Pond and Other Chilling Tales.* Philomel, 1987. 111pp.
Grades 3-5
Judith Gorog is a master at making stories twist and leaving unexpected endings for readers to ponder. Although it was published in 1982, try also *A Taste for Quiet: and Other Disquieting Tales* (Philomel).
1. The Sufficient Prayer: Sometimes, if you pray for death, it comes when you least desire it.
BL 06/15/87, KR 02/01/87

Gorog, Judith. *On Meeting Witches at Wells.* Philomel, 1991. 119pp. Grades 3-6
These are not horrific stories although they are cataloged as such in the CIP. They actually are different tales—some chilling and some wistful, but all thoughtful—told at a school sewing bee. A different member of the school community weaves each into the main framework of the book.
1. An Old, Often Retold Story of Revenge: A Chinese servant girl has had a clever revenge on her stingy foreign master.
KR 10/15/91, LA 11/92

Gorog, Judith. *Please Do Not Touch: A Collection of Stories.* Scholastic Inc., 1993. 131pp.
Grades 5-8
Designed as a tour of a gallery, this collection has more scary stories than Gorog's others, and they range from folktales to modern personal stories.
1. The coffeepot: The appliances in Rhoda's house have taken over, commanding her actions.

2. The Rented House: The last tenants were murderers, or were they murdered?
BL 10/01/93, KR 08/01/93

Gorog, Judith. *Three Dreams and A Nightmare: and Other Tales of the Dark.* Philomel, 1998. 156pp. Grades 6-8
    1. Mall Rat: When Rita doesn't lock her car doors, an unexpected, dangerous passenger shows up in the back seat.
    2. At the Sign of the Beckoning Finger: A young man is collecting all the items of a murder, including the remains.
    3. The Price of Magic: A creature tries to convince a boy to kill his mother.
    Reviews not available.

Greenberg, Martin H., Jill M. Morgan, and Robert Weinberg, eds. *Great Writers & Kids Write Spooky Stories.* Random House, 1995. Illustrator: Gahan Wilson. 224pp. Grades 5-7
    A great idea, combining the talents of well-known authors with their children (age 7-adult). This book is unique in design, with author's notes explain the processes used by each team.
    1. In Transit: A father and son reveal themselves to be traveling cannibals.
    2. Closet Monsters: Conquering her fear, a girl saves her mother from the monster in the closet.
    KR 04/01/95, SLJ 02/96

Greenberg, Martin, and Charles Waugh, eds. *A Newbery Halloween: Thirteen Scary Stories by Newbery-Award Winning Authors.* Delacorte, 1993. 189pp. Grade 4 & Up
    Written by award-winning authors, these 12 stories are taken from chapters of Newbery novels. Some stories ("The Baddest Witch in the World") are funny, some ("The Witch's Eye") are supernatural, and some ("The Year Halloween Happened One Day Early") are spooky.
    BL 09/01/93, SLJ 10/93

Griffiths, Barbara. *Frankenstein's Hamster: Ten Spine-Tingling Tales.* Dial, 1990. Illustrated by the author. 113pp. Grades 6-9
    Although the title and cover illustrations appeal to a younger audience, the sophisticated stories are meant for older readers.
    1. Frankenstein's Hamster: A twisted boy with no friends makes a classmate into his buddy, the Frankenstein way.
    Reviews not available.

Grinnel, George Bird, comp. John Bierhorst, ed. *The Whistling Skeleton: American Indian Tales of the Supernatural.* Scholastic, 1982. Illustrator: Robert Andrew Parker. 110pp. Grades 4-6
    Although this was published in 1982, it is a strong contribution. It includes not only stories but also historical notes written by Bierhorst, which provide great insight for understanding the Pawnee, the Blackfoot, and the Cheyenne.

1. The Stolen Girl: A girl believes she is marrying a man, but in the morning, she is surrounded only by rats.
2. Ghost Story: A girl escapes death by a witch but must then use magic to escape more peril.
3. The Boy Who Was Sacrificed: After a father kills his son, the boy is brought back to life by animals that teach him many powerful things.
   BL 02/01/83, SLJ 11/82

Haskins, James. *The Headless Haunt and Other African-American Ghost Stories*.
HarperCollins, 1994. Illustrator: Ben Otero. 115pp. Grades 4-6

These short stories and personal narratives explain the plat-eye (a ghost with one dangling eye), haunts, and other strange mysticisms common in African-American Folklore.

1. A Treasure-Hunting Story: A slave is frightened when the spirit of her former master comes back to reveal his gold.
   CBRS 10/94

Haskins, Jim. *Moaning Bones: African-American Ghost Stories*. Lothrop, Lee & Shepard, 1998.
Illustrator: Felicia Marshall. 61pp. Grades 3-6

These short stories contain no gore.

1. You Shot Me Once: The ghost of a dead man comes back to seek revenge, and the silver bullets of his killer offer no protection.
2. Old Hy-Ty: A murdered man's ghost comes back as a very tall haunt—so tall they call him Hy-Ty.
   CBRS 11/98, SLJ 12/98

Hill, Mary, ed. *Creepy Classics*. Random House, 1994. Illustrator: Dominick R. Domingo. 120pp.
Grades 5-7

These are classic stories, with introductions and a glossary that have been edited to appeal to the younger audiences. Included are "Dracula's Guest" (a Bram Stoker adaptation) and "Frankenstein Creates a Monster." This collection is not part of the Lowell House collections, which are unedited compilations.

1. The Dead Girl: This story, by Guy de Maupassant, is that of a man stricken with grief when his lover dies. He goes to the graveyard, and there, her deceitful nature is revealed.
   BL 10/15/94, SLJ 12/94

Hill, Susan, ed. *The Random House Book of Ghost Stories*. Random House, 1991. 223pp.
Grades 5-8

These 17 stories were written by English writers.

1. The Yellow Ball: Two children play ball with a ghost dog. When the ball is destroyed, it becomes a "ghost ball," which suits the dog fine.

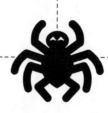

2. Laughter in the Dark: A miserly and miserable man gloats about his ability to make others grovel for money, but the last laugh is on him.
PW 08/30/91, LT 09/91

Hodges, Margaret. *Hauntings: Ghosts and Ghouls from Around the World*. Little, Brown, 1991. Illustrator: David Wenzel. 123pp. Grades 4-6

This collection contains 16 of the most common spooky folktales from around the world.
1. Godfather Death: The Brothers Grimm story of how Death allows his godson to become a great doctor until the godson tries to cheat death.
2. The Tinker and the Ghost: In this story of Esteban and the Ghost, a man stays the night at a haunted palace and is rewarded after helping the ghost of a murdered man.
KR 09/91

Jacques, Brian. *Seven Strange and Ghostly Tales*. Philomel, 1991. 137pp. Grades 5-8
Master storyteller Jacques shares tales of ghosts, vampires, and demons.
1. Jamie and the Vampires: This is a funny story of a boy, his mother, a dare, and some vampires.
SLJ 12/91, PW 08/16/91

Kallen, Stuart. *Ghosts of the Seven Seas*. Abdo & Daughters, 1991. Illustrator: Tim Blough. 32pp. Grades 2-5

Eight short stories for reluctant readers include simple text and drawings.
1. The Case of the Headless Sailor: The ship Squanto was haunted for years by a murdered sailor until no one would board it, and it sank in the Atlantic.
Reviews not available.

Knight, David C. *The Moving Coffins: Ghosts and Hauntings Around the World*. Prentice-Hall, 1983. Illustrator: Neil Waldman. 150pp. Grades 5-8

These well-crafted stories, typically three pages in length, details "documented" haunts of the world.
1. Dead Voices from a Haunted Tape Recorder: A Swedish artist was able to record the voices of people long dead, including Hitler and Napoleon.
BL 01/01/84, SLJ 03/84

Kunnas, Mauri, and Tarja Kunnas. *One Spooky Night and Other Scary Stories*. Crown, 1985. 42pp. Grades 1-4

In this oversized picture book, cartoon characters share silly stories such as "Old Nessie: The Loch Ness Monster and the Case of the Horrible Hiccups." Translated from the original Finnish publication.
PW 08/22/86

Leach, Maria. *The Thing at the Foot of the Bed and Other Scary Tales*. Putnam, 1987. Illustrator: Marc Simont. 126pp. Grades 2-6

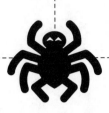

This classic book of traditional folktales includes:

1. Wait Till Martin Comes: A man is terrified at the thought of meeting the leader of wild cats.
2. The Golden Arm: You don't know jump tales if you don't know this classic.
3. I'm in the Room: "Up the stairs, in the room, I GOT YOU!"

Reviews not available.

Leach, Maria. *Whistle in the Graveyard*. Viking, 1974. Illustrator: Ken Rinciari. 128pp. Grades 4-6

I've included this collection of historical tales of spooks and spirits because it seems to be a staple in most library collections.

1. Anne Boleyn: The executed wife of King Henry VIII returns to claim her innocence.
2. One Handful: A man's greed is revealed when he tells the story of how he tried to take not one, but two handfuls of treasure.

Reviews not available.

Lewis, Shari, and Lan O'Kun. *One-Minute Scary Stories*. Doubleday, 1991. Illustrators: Pat and Robin DeWitt. 48pp. Grades 3-4

Part of the *One-Minute* series, these are short adaptations of stories, including "The Legend of Sleepy Hollow," "Dr. Jekyll and Mr. Hyde," and "The Monkey's Paw." Each story is told on a two-page spread with illustrations.

HBG Spring 1992

Lively, Penelope. *Uninvited Ghosts and Other Stories*. Dutton, 1985. Illustrator: John Lawrence. 120pp. Grades 5-7

The only ghost story in this collection is from the title "Uninvited Ghosts."

1. Time Trouble: A clock makes a mysterious deal with a boy who would give anything to relive his wonderful afternoon.

BL 06/15/85, KR 05/15/85

Lonsdale, Pamela, ed. *Spooky Stories of the Supernatural*. Prentice Hall, 1985. Illustrator: Joanna Carey. 143pp. Grades 6-8

This is a collection of seven lengthy stories written by English authors.

1. In a Dark, Dark Box: As it is being told, a story comes to life, frightening and confusing a boy.

BL 06/15/85, SLJ 08/85

Low, Alice, comp. *Spooky Stories for a Dark and Stormy Night*. Hyperion, 1994. Illustrator: Gahan Wilson. 125pp. Grades 3-6

Both traditional folktales and current stories are compiled in a book with cartoon illustrations.

1. Uninvited Ghosts: Penelope Lively's story involves two children who make a deal with

the family of ghosts that are annoying them and pass them off to two unsuspecting babies.
2. Rap! Rap! Rap!: Up the stairs on a dark and stormy night, the man found…wrapping paper!
3. Bedtime Snacks: Laurence Yep's slightly gruesome story tells of a hungry monster that eats a child before being outwitted by his brother.
BL 10/01/94, LT 11/94

Lunn, Janet, comp. *The Unseen: Scary Stories*. Puffin Books, 1994. 170pp. Grade 6 & Up
Some of these stories, written by Canadian authors, are too sophisticated for the average elementary-age child. One story, "Carrot Cake," makes explicit, gruesome reference to the *Psycho* movies.
1. The Closet: Uncle Gus keeps an unburied skeleton in his closet, and Jeremy and his dad dig a grave for it.
2. The Return of Hester: The ghost of her sister gives permission for a woman to marry.
CM 11/94

Lyons, Mary. *Raw Head, Bloody Bones: African American Tales of the Supernatural*. Macmillan, 1991. 86pp. Grade 5 & Up
Told in Gullah ('Gola) speech with notes on sources, these 15 stories include giants, ghouls, ogres, and ghosts from African folklore.
1. Raw Head, Devil and the Barefoot Woman: The Devil relies on a woman's help to break up a loving couple.
2. Dead Aaron: "The Dancing Skeleton" is told in Gullah dialect.
BL 01/01/92, KR 10/15/91

MacDonald, Caroline. *Hostilities: Nine Bizarre Stories*. Scholastic, 1991. 131pp. Grades 6-9
Sophisticated readers will enjoy these truly bizarre stories that will haunt the mind for a long time.
1. Dandelion Creek: A séance brings forth a fright that warns campers of the real danger awaiting them in the woods.
2. Hostilities: A stepbrother and sister find ways to torture one another, ranging from mild annoyances to a near-death experience.
Magpies 7/91

Macklin, John. *World's Most Bone-Chilling "True" Ghost Stories*. Sterling, 1993. Illustrator: Jim Sharpe. 96pp. Grade 5 & Up
These stories are certainly scary and hopefully *not* true!
1. When Death Comes on Swift Wings: A mummy case brings death to anyone who owns it.
2. Did Michael Norton Fall Through a Hole in Time?: His voice can be heard, but his body is never found.

3. Killer Tree of the Cameroons: A body-crunching tree killed for years before being burned to the ground.
BL 09/01/94, HBG Spring 1994

McDonald, Collin. *The Chilling Hour: Tales of the Real and Unreal.* Cobblehill, 1992. 153pp. Grades 6-8
More "chilling" than the author's first collection, *Nightwaves*, this collection includes a story of a psychotic substitute teacher determined to kill students for their parents' wrongs.
1. The Driver: After a blizzard, a father is able to save his family from accepting a ride with a driver he recognizes as Death.
2. The Mailbox: An antique mailbox delivers notes concerning the health and future of residents.
KR 07/15/92, SLJ 08/92

McDonald, Collin. *Nightwaves: Scary Tales for After Dark.* Cobblehill, 1990. 112pp. Grades 5-8
This is the author's first book of original horror stories.
1. The Radio: Bored one summer, Tom builds a radio that can predict the future. Unfortunately, he doesn't hear the prediction of his own death.
2 The Dam: A dangerous class trip leads to the death of a school girl, and the horrid memory of the incident for a grown woman.
BL 10/1/90, KR 8/1/90

McDonald, Collin. *Shadows and Whispers: Tales from the Other Side.* Cobblehill, 1994. 135pp. Grades 5-8
Time travel and dream stories blur the lines between reality and imagined terror.
1. The Slumber Party: Girls view a mysterious movie that reveals the murder of a projection booth operator. But was it a dream?
2. Souvenirs: While bored on vacation, cousin Jeff disappears and is later seen as a tiny statue in the souvenir shop.
BL 09/01/94

McKean, Tom. *Into the Candlelit Room and Other Strange Tales.* Putnam, 1999. 215pp. Grades 5-8
These are five well-crafted stories that are shared in unusual formats, such as journal entries and a college entrance essay.
1. Into the Candlelit Room: The son of a poor, Polish immigrant wishes to be rich, and he almost makes a deal with the devil.
2. Caring: A girl explains how, in spite of the mysterious deaths that have occurred around her, she manages to be the caring student desired by an upstanding college.
BL 07/01/99, BR 01/00

McKissack, Patricia. *The Dark-Thirty: Southern Tales of the Supernatural.* Knopf, 1992. Illustrator: Brian Pinkney. 122pp. Grades 4-8

> This collection includes ten stories and an informative author's note.
>
> 1. The 11:59: Any porter who hears the whistle of the 11:59 train has 24 hours until death arrives.
> 2. The Woman in the Snow: After a bigoted bus driver refuses to bring a woman and her child to the hospital, he suffers an "accidental" death.
>
> SLJ 11/92, PW 09/07/92

Medearis, Angela Shelf. *Haunts: Five Hair-Raising Tales.* Holiday House, 1996. Illustrator: Trina Schart Hyman. 37pp. Grades 4-6

> These original stories contain black-and-white drawings.
>
> 1. Scared Silly: Not a silly story, this is an account of a headless horseman come back to haunt bold young girls.
>
> BL 02/01/97, KR 11/01/96

Moser, Barry, comp. *Great Ghost Stories.* William Morrow, 1988. Illustrator: Barry Moser. 200pp. Grades 5-8

> Ghost stories for the upper-level students as written by H. G. Wells, Madeline L'Engle, and Joyce Carol Oates. Moser provides one illustration per story.
>
> 1. The Others: A man is troubled when he sees what he believes must be ghosts of people long deceased. Later, he finds himself moving through a long tunnel of faceless people.
>
> Reviews not available.

Nixon, Joan Lowery. *Ghost Town: Seven Ghostly Stories.* Delacorte, 2000. 147pp. Grades 4-8

> This collection of encounters about kids and ghosts is followed by factual information concerning the ghost town. Travel directions and Web sites are included.
>
> 1. The Shoot-out. A boy meets the ghost of Billy Clanton, who teaches him a thing or two about Doc Holliday and the Earps before disappearing in a Tombstone shootout.
>
> BL 9/1/00, SLJ 10/00

Olson, Arielle and Howard Schwartz. *Ask the Bones: Scary Stories from Around the World.* Viking, 1999. Illustrator: David Linn. 132pp. Grade 5 & Up

> Many of these 22 creepy tales with source notes have been salvaged from out-of-print materials. They are definitely horrifying.
>
> 1. Beginning with the Ears: A wife warns of a witch's plan to kill and eat the family, beginning with the man's ears.
> 2. Fiddling with Fire: A man sells his soul to the devil in order to play the fiddle.
> 3. A Night of Terror: Witches trap two rabbinical students.
> 4. The Black Snake: A giant gruesomely kills two merchants with a snake.
>
> BL 05/01/99, BR 09/99

Park, Ruth. *Things in Corners.* Viking, 1989. 197pp. Grades 6-9

Although they are not scary, these stories are lengthy and unnerving for the patient reader. Ruth Park is Australian, so some terms may need to be defined.

    1. Getting through Saturday: When a girl decides to ruin her family's vacation, her brother must save her in the wilderness. They discover skeletal remains and a secret that bonds them forever.

    2. What kind of lady was Auntie Bev? Auntie Bev was the kind of lady who would send a guardian spirit to keep watch over her house and her prized possessions.

    GP 5/90, EL 3/90

Pearce, Philippa. *Who's Afraid? And Other Strange Stories.* Greenwillow, 1986. 152pp. Grades 5-8

This collection of 11 stories from England is shivery, but not horrific.

    1. Black Eyes: The cousin of a girl believes her teddy bear has the power to inflict ill upon those who upset her.

    2. Who's Afraid?: During a game of hide and seek, Granny comes to the rescue for Joe, whom Cousin Dicky would kill if he could.

    BL 4/1/87, SLJ 5/87

Pepper, Dennis, ed. *The Oxford Book of Scary Tales.* Oxford University Press, 1992. 156pp. Grade 5 & Up

These are deliciously spooky stories and poems.

    1. Crossing Over: Does the dog or the girl die in the car accident?

    2. Camilla: During an "interview," the author reveals her encounter with a dead friend who appeared alive at her birthday party.

    3. My Great-Grandfather's Grave Digging: A funny "true" story of a talking grave.

    BL 01/15/93, KR 11/01/92

Peters, Andrew Fusek. *Strange and Spooky Stories.* Millbrook, 1997. 78pp. Grades 3-5

Very few of these stories are spooky, and many are fables from around the world.

    1. The Woman Who Tricked Death: A woman tells a boring story to Death, thus putting him to sleep and saving her own life.

    Reviews not available.

Powling, Chris, ed. *Faces in the Dark: A Book of Scary Stories.* Kingfisher, 1994. Illustrator: Peter Bailey. 80pp. Grades 3-6

Eight of the ten stories are original works, and all are meant to be read aloud.

    1. A Face in the Dark: A professor is frightened when the members of his community appear with no facial features.

    2. A Loathly Lady: A cruel hag turns into a queen, but could she ever turn back? A great description of the hag, includes, "Red with blood her eyes were, with crusts of yellow

matter at the corners, and the lower lids sagged to show wet, red linings."
BL 01/01/95, LT 01/95

Price, Susan, comp. *Horror Stories: A Spine-Chilling Collection.* Kingfisher, 1995. Illustrator: Harry Horse. 255pp. Grades 6-9

If you are like most of us, Stephen King is not in your collection. So fans will be delighted that one of his stories, mild as it is, sneaked into this collection. Most of the stories are horrific; some are classics, and one ("The Famous Five Go Pillaging") was discontinued by the publishers.

1. Here There Be Tygers: In this King story, a boy is afraid to use the basement bathroom at his school for fear of attack by the feline.
2. Something: Something dark and foreboding which will take them from this life awaits a boy and all the men in his family.

BL 10/15/95

Richardson, Jean, comp. *Beware! Beware! Chilling Tales.* Viking Kestrel, 1989. 120pp. Grades 5-8

The best English authors contributed to this collection of stark, grim tales.

1. How Does Your Garden Grow?: A girl does not realize the strength in her witchcraft until she kills her neighbor and must ask her grandmother for help.
2. Nightmare: A boy's best friend returns from the dead on a horse that causes nightmares.

BL 6/1/89, SLJ 3/89

Russell, Jean, ed. *Supernatural Stories: 13 Tales of the Unexpected.* Orchard, 1987. 155pp. Grades 5-8

These stories were written by authors from the United Kingdom.

1. The Dollmaker: Girls visit a woman to have their dolls repaired and later find that their new classmate has been composed entirely of beautiful doll features.
2. Spring-heeled Jack: A girl unearths a misplaced gargoyle that has been causing fear in the neighborhood.

BL 09/01/87, SLJ 09/87

Salway, Lance. *A Nasty Piece of Work and Other Ghost Stories.* Clarion, 1985. Illustrator: Jeremy Ford. 128pp. Grades 5-8

Some of these seven original stories are quite unnerving.

1. Such a Sweet Little Girl: A girl summons "her" ghost to attack brother Edward.
2. Pretty Penny: Envied by her sister, Penny is murdered, but she eternally haunts her sister's mind.
3. A Nasty Piece of Work: Martin is given a witch stick to convince him of the reality of ghosts, and his encounter results in a mass attack by flies.

BL 09/01/85, SLJ 09/85

Schwartz, Alvin. *More Scary Stories to Tell in the Dark.* HarperCollins, 1984. Illustrator: Stephen Gammell. 100pp. Grade 4 & Up

These traditional folktales and urban legends are wildly popular with Stephen Gammell's illustrations.

1. One Sunday Morning: Ida wonders whether a church service full of dead people was real or not.
2. Wonderful Sausage: As children disappear and a butcher goes mad, villagers delight in wonderful sausage.
3. The Voice: "Ellen, I'm coming to get you!"
4. The Bed by the Window: An old man in a hospital kills his roommate so that he can have the bed by the window.
BL 03/01/85, SLJ 02/85

Schwartz, Alvin. *Scary Stories 3: More Tales to Chill Your Bones.* HarperCollins, 1991. Illustrator: Stephen Gammell. 115pp. Grade 4 & Up 📼

Just what the title says.

1. Harold: This is a somewhat gruesome account of a scarecrow's revenge on two farmers.
2. The Dead Hand: Another haunting lesson is learned too late one night in the swamps.
3. T-h-u-p-p-p-p-p! A ghost taunts a girl and finally gives her a "raspberry."
BL 08/91, KR 07/01/91

Schwartz, Alvin. *Scary Stories to Tell in the Dark.* HarperCollins, 1986. Illustrator: Stephen Gammell. 111pp. Grade 4 & Up 📼

This collection of folktales retold by the author is one of the most banned books in the elementary field.

1. The Big Toe: A boy digs up a toe and makes a stew, but the owner of the toe comes to claim his appendage.
2. The Wendigo: This is a Native American legend.
3. Dead Man's Brains: I've never found kids naive enough to believe this, but it's always fun at Halloween.
4. The Hook: This urban legend involves a teenage couple who narrowly escape the attack of a man with a hook for his hand.
BL 12/01/86, Book Links 01/01/98

Shanan, Sherry. *Wait Until Dark: Seven Scary Sleepover Stories.* Bantam, 1996. 104pp. Grades 3-5

These are the stories that rely on cheap thrills and ridiculous scenarios.

1. Fat Chance: A girl with a weight problem is encouraged to seek revenge on her persecutors. She stomps the earth and creates a quake that kills them.
Reviews not available.

Sonntag, Linda, comp. *The Ghost Story Treasury*. Putnam, 1987. Illustrator: Annabel Spenceley. 93pp. Grades 3-5

> 15 stories and poems are contained in this collection.
> 1. The Guitarist: a man lends his guitar to a great player, who in the end says, "You should have heard me when I was alive!"
> 2. A Story About Death: Mama tricks Death so that he doesn't steal her baby.
> KR 10/01/07, PW 10/25/87

Speregen, Devra N. *Scary Stories to Drive You Batty*. Watermill Press, 1995. 46pp. Grades 3-4

These three chilling stories are perfectly written for eight- and nine-year-olds. They won't drive anyone batty, but they may raise a few goosebumps.

> 1. Truth or Scare: A new kid in town has a tendency to brag and is challenged by the neighborhood children to spend time alone in the haunted house his parents just purchased.
> Reviews not available.

Stamper, J. B. *Night Frights: Thirteen Scary Stories*. Scholastic, 1993. 75pp. Grades 3-5

Somewhere between the Alvin Schwartz *Scary Stories* and Robert San Souci's *Short and Shivery*, lies *Night Frights*. These are hybrid works—part folktale, part original adaptations—that are short and spooky.

> 1. Bloody Mary: After hearing the story at a sleepover, Mary is compelled to conjure the spirit.
> 2. The Corpse's Revenge: In this adaptation of "Buried Alive," Harry thwarts his grave robbers and walks home.
> Reviews not available.

Stamper, J. B. *Still More Night Frights: Thirteen Scary Stories*. Scholastic, 1996. 90pp. Grades 3-5

This collection of stories adapted from folklore has been modernized and is aimed at the intermediate readers.

> 1. The Club: Ghosts try to entice a new boy in town to join their club of the undead.
> 2. Horrorscope: Although she tries to avoid her fate, a girl is run over by a car after she reads her warning horoscope.
> Reviews not available.

Starkey, Dinah. *Ghosts and Bogles*. Heinemann, 1985. Illustrator: Jan Pienkowski. 123pp. Grades 5-6

From England, come these 16 stories of various haunts and specters. Not scary, but told in English style, the stories contain some vocabulary that may be confusing to younger children.

> 1. The Boggart of Castle Farm: A ghost that is accustomed to cream, turns up his nose

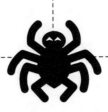

when offered skim milk, and the family just can't get rid of him.
GP 01/86, SL 03/86

Stearns, Michael, ed. *A Nightmare's Dozen: Stories From the Dark*. Harcourt, 1996.
Illustrator: Michael Hussar. 239pp. Grades 6-9

This is one of the best collections I've read. Full of nightmare material, the stories are a mixture of fantasy, horror, and mystery. All are scary, yet appropriate for this audience.

1. Cypress Swamp Granny: A vain girl seeks the help of a conjure woman to bring her wealth and love, but the help comes at a price.
2. Mrs. Pomeroy: This story is a bad student's worst nightmare. A teacher scares her students into good behavior by using her witchcraft to switch their bodies into her own.
BL 1/97, SLJ 12/96

Vande Velde, Vivian. *Curses, Inc. and Other Stories*. Harcourt, 1997. 226pp. Grades 5-8

This is one of the better collections I have read. It consists of ten great stories about witches.

1. Curses, Inc.: A boy wants to put a spell on a classmate by placing an order through an Internet site. The story is told in both prose and online screen messages.
2. Past Sunset: In France, there is a town where people know the rules; by day, children run carefree, but at night they must be home to avoid the ghostly woman who will steal their souls with a look in her eyes.
CCB-B 5/97, KR 2/15/97

Vivelo, Jackie. *Chills in the Night: Tales That will Haunt You*. DK Ink., 1997. Illustrator: Jennifer Eachus. 123pp. Grade 5 & Up

These eight original, smart stories will make you shiver.

1. When There's Nothing There at All: Living in a house that was once a funeral home can be terribly frightening, especially when your family disappears in the night.
2. The Fireside Book of Ghost Stories: A haunted book wills its readers to pursue stories that may save their lives.
BL 01/01/98, LT 05/98

Vivelo, Jackie. *Chills Run Down My Spine*. DK Ink, 1995. Illustrator: Jennifer Eachus. 125pp.
Grade 5 & Up

These nine original spine-tinglers are sure to please the upper grades.

1. Cradle Song: An only child gets a new brother, Ben, whose wolf identity is not revealed until the last passage of the story.
2. Chills Run Down My Spine: On Halloween, a boy is locked in an abandoned house, haunted by a spirit that suffered the same fate 40 years ago.
3. The Bell Ringer: Hope's cousin Boyd can murder people just by wishing them dead.
BL 11/15/94, SLJ 12/94

Whitcher, Susan. *Real Mummies Don't Bleed: Friendly Tales for October Nights.* Farrar, 1993. Illustrator: Andrew Glass. 119pp. Grades 3-6

These stories are a safe choice for those who want to provide stories involving mystery and adventure with slight suspense. They are not for the die-hard fans of fear.

1. Mystery of the One-Eyed Dog: Men disappear while dogs accumulate at Miss Dulcie's house, home of the famous coconut cake.

HBG Spring 1994, SLJ 02/94

Wood, Ted. *Ghosts of the Southwest: The Phantom Gunslinger and Other Real-Life Hauntings.* Walker, 1997. 49pp. Grades 3-6

Some of the most well known ghosts in America may be found in hotels, inns, and other public places. Ted Wood cleverly photographs people in transparent images to give a haunted effect and includes a short story with each.

BL 03/01/97, LT 05/97

Wood, Ted. *Ghosts of the West Coast: The Lost Souls of the Queen Mary, and Other Real Life Hauntings.* Walker, 1999. 48pp. Grades 3-6

These "Haunted America" books are fantastic, not only for the full-page color photographs but also for the short stories that accompany them.

BL 04/15/99, SLJ 06/01/99

Wyeth, Sharon Dennis. *Vampire Bugs: Stories Conjured from the Past.* Delacorte, 1995. Illustrator: Curtis James 80pp. Grades 4-6

Six short stories range in topic from voodoo masters to slave times. Unfamiliar words are defined at the end of each story.

1. Vampire Bugs: A witch and her children are shrunken to become today's fireflies.

BL 01/01/95, HBG Fall 1995

Yamamoto, Neal. *Scary Myths and Legends from Around the World.* Lowell House, 1997. Illustrator: Matthew Nelson. 89pp. Grades 4-6

Concise stories with historical notes, bibliography and index.

1. The Black Spider: In this tale from Switzerland, a man makes a deal with the devil, who comes for revenge in the form of a deadly spider.
2. The Golden Arm: This classic jump tale has been revised, giving it a haunting, unfinished ending.

Reviews not available.

Yashinsky, Dan, comp. *Ghostwise: A Book of Midnight Stories.* August House, 1997. 224pp. Grades 3-6

Some collections are so wonderful that I have to buy them immediately upon reading. This is one of those collections—organized so that even the most timid reader can avoid the "maximum nightmare" material of one chapter.

1. The Story of the Boogie-Woman: If you have third and fourth graders, tell them this story. It is perfect for the age level, and one of the most entertaining stories I have come across. The boogie woman is a really big monster, and she likes to eat naughty children.
2. Room for One More: This story for upper-level children tells how a man dodges his death by listening to a dream.
3. A Duppy Tale: A disobedient boy kills a magic bird and pays the consequences.
VOYA 02/98, Kliatt 11/97

Yolen, Jane. *Here There Be Ghosts.* Harcourt, 1998. 122pp. Grades 4-8
These original stories and poems include short introductions by the author.
1. Police Report: Friends are warned to remove themselves from the tomb of an angry old ghost.
2. Mandy: As she is dying, the spirit of a loyal dog comes to the aid of her owner, who is miserable at camp.
BL 11/01/98, SLJ 11/98

Yolen, Jane. *Here There Be Witches.* Harcourt, 1995. Illustrator: David Wilgus. 117pp. Grades 4-8
Perfect for a dark and spooky night, these creepy and disturbing poems and stories are for more mature audiences.
1. Circles: A girl wishes her father not to die…and he doesn't.
2. Weird Sisters: This poem is a tribute to a childhood friend whose parents were alcoholic and suicidal.
BL 10/15/95, SLJ 12/95

Yolen, Jane, ed. *The Haunted House: A Collection of Original Stories.* HarperCollins, 1995. Illustrators: Martin Greenberg and Doron Ben-Ami. 85pp. Grades 3-6
Seven authors describe seven family situations at the same house at 66 Brown's End.
1. The Gourmet Ghost: A very fat ghost has an insatiable appetite.
2. And the Lights Flickered: After trying to scare one another, two boys see a hand emerge from the shower.
BL 09/95, SLJ 11/95

Yolen, Jane, ed. *Things That Go Bump in the Night: A Collection of Original Stories.* Harper & Row, 1989. 276pp. Grades 5-8
This collection includes stories written by William Sleator, Bruce Coville, and others. Some of the stories will keep you up at night!
1. The Baby-Sitter: Hilary laughs off the magic the twins do to keep "them" away, but in a babysitting nightmare, an intruder suffers his fate at the hands of "them."

2. Ghost Dancers: In a two-page story, a brother and sister watch ghosts dance on Halloween night.
BL 10/01/89, SLJ 10/89

Yolen, Jane, ed. *Vampires: A Collection of Original Stories*. Harpercollins, 1991. 228pp. Grade 6 & Up

Remembering that the vampire is the sexiest of the undead, this is a book for older readers. Co-edited with Martin Greenberg.

1. Nobody Has to Know: Two nameless students discuss the possibility of one becoming a vampire.
2. Ahvel: A young boy-turned-vampire must be put to rest gently.
BL 03/15/92, SLJ 11/91

Yolen, Jane, and Martin H. Greenberg, eds. *Werewolves: A Collection of Original Stories*. Harper & Row, 1988. 271pp. Grades 5-8

This collection includes 15 stories ranging from mild to terrifying.

1. Night Calls: After a wolf hunt, four men are revealed to have become werewolves; one is the brother of the narrator.
2. Monster Mash: Knowing that the full moon coincides with his band's all-important concert, a boy makes a decision that almost creates a monster "mash."
BL 07/88, SLJ 09/88

Young, Judy Dockrey, and Richard Young. *Favorite Scary Stories of American Children*. August House, 1990. Illustrator: Wendell E. Hall. 110pp. Grades 3-6

This collection includes 23 of the most famous stories, with notes for use. An informative afterward gives support for sharing scary stories.

1. Bloody Mary, Bloody Mary: Children love to conjure Bloody Mary, and this version is mild, without specific details.
2. The Hobbyahs: This tale is about a little dog that saves his family by barking at the goblins that are looking for dinner.
BL 12/01/90, SLJ 03/91

Young, Judy Dockrey and Richard Young. *Ozark Ghost Stories*. August House, 1995. 154pp. Grades 5-8

These stories from the people who live in the Ozark region of Arkansas and Missouri includes an informative introduction, notes, and a glossary.

1. Pennywinkle! Pennywinkle!: This story and *Blood Red Cedar* are versions of "The Singing Bone" story, in which the stepmother kills and cooks her stepson. The father eats the child, but his spirit rises to sing the truth, which brings revenge and justice.
BL 6/1/95, PW 5/29/95

Young, Richard, and Judy Dockrey Young. *Ghastly Ghost Stories*. Random House, 1993.
Grades 5-8

This collection is simply the combination of two books, *Ghost Stories from the American Southwest* and *Ghost Stories from the American South*, both by the Youngs. The only problem with this collection is that you can't put it down. The stories are so vast and appealing that they consume you until you have completed them. See individual books for recommendations.
Reviews not available.

Young, Richard, and Judy Dockrey Young. *Ghost Stories from the American South*. August
House, 1990. Grades 4-8

The introduction to this book gives great insight as to why and how these tales are told. The tales themselves are brief narratives and are grouped according to theme.
1. Raw Head and Bloody Bones: This is the story of a pig turned into a man who comes back after being slaughtered.
2. You Can't Get Out: A drunk falls into a freshly-dug grave and is scared by a young man who also had fallen in.
Kliatt 9/93

Young, Richard, and Judy Dockrey Young. *Ghost Stories from the American Southwest*.
August House, 1991. 190pp. Grades 6-8

Divided into sections, including Ghost Jokes, Urban Legends, Ghostly Lights, Ghosts of the Roadways, Haunted Houses, and Other Haunted Places, this book contains excellent source notes and an index of stories by state of origin.
1. The Haunted Car: A humorous story of a preacher who takes a ride in a car with no driver. Believing it is haunted, he warns a man not to go near it and is surprised to find that the phantom driver was actually the owner who had pushed the car from behind.
Reviews not available.

Young, Richard, and Judy Dockrey Young. *The Scary Story Reader: Forty-one of the Scariest
Stories for Sleepovers, Campfires, Car and Bus Trips—Even for First Dates!* August House,
1993. 174pp. Grades 5-8

This book of graphic urban legends includes an introduction by Jan Harold Brunvand.
1. But I'm Not!: This version of "The Freshman Initiation" involves a simple prank that turns to death and madness for college students who spend the night in an abandoned house.
2. Bloody Fingers: In terror, a man tries to escape a skeletal figure that simply wants to play tag.
3. 11:11: This warning time for students reminds them not to drink and drive.
BL 11/15/93, SLJ 05/94

Poetry and Riddles

Bennett, Jill. *Spooky Poems*. Little, Brown, 1989. Illustrator: Mary Rees. Grades K-4
This book contains 24 spooky, original poems, including "Hairy Toe" and "Alphabet Monster."
KR 10/01/89

Brown, Marc. *Scared Silly: A Book for the Brave*. Little, Brown, 1994. Illustrated by the author. Grades 1-3
This is a collection of funny poems from many different authors, including Judith Viorst and Ogden Nash. Marc Brown's illustrations are complimentary, adding to the humor and enhancing the jokes and epitaphs.
PW 07/04/94, SLJ 09/94

Clarke, Gillian, comp. *The Whispering Room: Haunted Poems*. Kingfisher, 1996. Illustrator: Justin Todd. 68pp. Grades 3-6
This collection of illustrated poems by various authors includes "The Bogeyman" by Jack Prelutsky, "Ariel's Song" by Shakespeare, and "Spellbound" by Emily Bronte.
HBG Spring 1997, SLJ 12/96

Evans, Dilys. *Monster Soup and Other Spooky Poems*. Scholastic, 1992. Illustrator: Jacqueline Rogers. Grades 1-5
These mildly spooky poems cover the common Halloween cast: witches, monsters, and ghosts.
BL 08/92, SLJ 10/92

Florian, Douglas. *Monster Motel*. Harcourt, 1993. Illustrated by the author. Grades K-3
Goofy monsters live in the motel, including Sneaky Beeky, who may be hiding in your nose.
BL 03/15/93, SLJ 0/93

Gordon, Jeffie Ross. *Hide and Shriek: Riddles About Ghosts & Goblins*. Lerner, 1991. Illustrator: Susan Slattery Gordon. Grades 2-5
As the title indicates, these are riddles about ghosts and goblins.
BL 11/01/91, HGB Spring 1992

Hall, Katy and Lisa Eisenberg. *Boo Who? And Other Wicked Halloween Knock-Knock Jokes*. Harperfestival, 2000. Illustrator: Stephen Gammell. 16pp. Grades K-3
In this lift-the-flap book, readers find the answers to goofy knock-knocks under unusual pumpkins, bats, and goblins.

Hall, Katy and Lisa Eisenberg. *Creepy Riddles*. Dial, 1998. Illustrator: S.D. Schindler. Grades K-3

This title is part of the riddle collection by the author/illustrator team. It contains my favorite riddle: What did the zombie eat after he had a tooth taken out? (The dentist!)
BL 09/15/98, SLJ 10/98

Hall, Katy, and Lisa Eisenberg. *Mummy Riddles.* Dial, 1997. Illustrator: Nicole Rubel. 48pp. Grades K-3
This collection is funny from cover to cover, with puns and silly jokes, such as "What did the doctor tell the little mummy at her check up?" (You grue-some.)
BL 08/97, SLJ 11/97

Hall, Katy, and Lisa Eisenberg. *Trick or Eeek! And Other Ha Ha Halloween Riddles.* Illustrator: R.W. Alley. HarperCollins, 1996. 16pp. Grades K-3
Lifting the flaps, the readers get answers to silly jokes and riddles.

Heide, Florence Parry. *Grim and Ghastly Goings-On.* Lothrop, 1992. Illustrator:Victoria Chess. Grades 1-4
These 21 monster poems are mildly scary.
BL 09/15/92, SLJ 10/92

Himmelman, John. *I'm Not Scared!* Scholastic, 1994. Illustrated by the author. Grades K-2
I'm not scared reading these poems, and you won't be either. The subject matter includes a trip to the dentist, a bumblebee, and two classmates, among others. Only two poems actually deal with nighttime fears.
Reviews not available.

Hopkins, Lee Bennett. *Ragged Shadows: Poems of Halloween Night.* Little, Brown, 1993. Illustrator: Giles Laroche. 32pp. Grades K-4
These 14 poems are fun, not frightening.
BL 08/93, SLJ 09/93

Hopkins, Lee Bennett. *Creatures.* Harcourt, 1985. Illustrator: Stella Ormai. Grades 2-5
No need to be afraid of these 18 lighthearted poems.
BL 05/15/85, SLJ 04/85

Hubbell, Patricia. *Boo! Halloween Poems and Limericks.* Marshall Cavendish, 1988. Illustrator: Jeff Spackman. 40pp. Grades 2-5
These limericks can be enjoyed at the younger levels, but most of the poems offer just enough "creepiness" to satisfy an older audience as well. The illustrations are large and comical—a cross between MAD magazine and Tedd Arnold's work.
Reviews not available.

Keller, Charles. *Count Draculations! Monsters Riddles.* Prentice Hall, 1986. Illustrator: Edward Fascino. Grades 2-6
This collection of goofy riddles is great for Halloween or fun times.
BL 07/86, SLJ 10/86

Livingston, Myra Cohn. *Halloween Poems.* Holiday House, 1989. Illustrator: Stephen Gammell. 32pp. Grades 2-5

Sometimes you have to wonder what torments Stephen Gammell's mind: His illustrations are creepier than the 18 poems.

BL 09/15/89, SLJ 09/89

McNaughton, Colin. *Making Friends with Frankenstein: A Book of Monstrous Poems and Pictures.* Candlewick, 1994. Illustrated by the author. 90pp. Grades 2-6

Gross but cheerful, this collection of approximately 50 poems is appealing to readers. The illustrations are cartoonish, and the poems make use of puns and humor in short, simple stanzas.

BL 05/15/94, SLJ 05/94

Maestro, Giulio. *More Halloween Howls: Riddles That Come Back to Haunt You.* Dutton, 1992. Illustrated by the author. Grades 2-5

These 58 riddles, one per page, include bright illustrations.

BL 06/15/92, SLJ 08/92

Prelutsky, Jack. *The Headless Horseman Rides Tonight: More Poems to Trouble Your Sleep.* Greenwillow, 1980. Illustrator: Arnold Lobel. 37pp. Grades 3-6

These poems are creepy, with dark illustrations to add to the mystery. A favorite of fourth graders is "The Invisible Beast," "…for although you cannot see it, it can see you very well."

Prelutsky, Jack. *Monday's Troll.* Greenwillow, 1996. Illustrator: Peter Sis. 39pp. Grades 2-5

Most of these 17 poems are silly, and Peter Sis's illustrations add subtly to the humor in "We're Seven Grubby Goblins" and "Mother Ogre's Lullaby."

BL 4/15/96, SLJ 4/96

Prelutsky, Jack. *Nightmares: Poems to Trouble Your Sleep.* Greenwillow, 1976. Illustrator: Arnold Lobel. Grades 3-6

These poems are well-known by most intermediate-aged children. They involve various mutant creatures prowling the grounds in search of children to eat.

Reviews not available.

Rosenbloom, Joseph. *Spooky Riddles and Jokes.* Sterling, 1987. Sanford Hoffman. Grades 2-6

The jokes are ridiculous, with some being "written" by silly make-believe authors, but it's all in good fun.

BL 11/01/87

Yolen, Jane. *Best Witches: Poems for Halloween.* Putnam, 1989. Illustrator: Elise Primavera. 48pp. Grades 3-6

Dark, full-page paintings accompany these 21 thought-provoking poems along the lines of nature and a witch's role.

BL 09/15/89, LT 09/89

Series

This section includes sets, such as *Goosebumps*, and any set of four books or more based on the same characters or set in the same place. Trilogies can be found in the novel section.

Ahlberg, Janet, and Allan Ahlberg. *Funnybones*. Greenwillow. Illustrated by the authors. Grades K-1

These are simple picture books that feature a big skeleton, a little skeleton, and a skeleton dog who find adventure and mischief in their bony lives. Other titles include *The Black Cat, The Pet Shop, Dinosaur Dreams, Mystery Tour*, and *The Ghost Train*.

Arnold, Tedd. *Huggly*. Scholastic Cartwheel. Illustrated by the author. Kindergarten

The *Huggly* books are about a cute, little monster named, you guessed it, Huggly. Huggly appears in *Monster Under the Bed, Huggly's Sleepover*, and *Huggly Gets Dressed*.

Bellairs, John. *The House with a Clock in Its Walls*. Dial. 179pp. Grades 4-7 🔲

This title, along with *The Letter, the Witch and the Ring*, was reprinted by Puffin Books in 1993. Brad Strickland helped to complete two titles, *A Figure in the Shadows* and *The Ghost in the Mirror*, which then set the novels into a series, entitled *The Puffin Chillers*. These are suspenseful stories, not too scary, and similar to Harry Potter. They are full of magic, wizardry, and sorcery. Rose Rita, her best friend Lewis, Mrs. Zimmerman (a good witch), and Uncle Jonathan battle evil with gratifying results.

Black, J. R. *Shadow Zone Series*. Bullseye Books, Random House. 128pp. Grades 4-6.

In each story, a teen encounters and survives a horror, such as living next door to a witch or fighting a computer phantom. Titles include *One Slimy Summer* and *Guess Who's Dating a Werewolf?*

Bullseye Chillers. Various authors and illustrators. Random House. 90pp. Grades 2-6

If you have readers who would like to read the classics but cannot comprehend the sophisticated language, try this series. It includes *Edgar Allan Poe's Tales of Terror, Frankenstein, The Phantom of the Opera,* and others.

Choose Your Own Nighmare. Various authors and illustrators. Bantam. 84pp. Grades 3-4

This interactive series allows the reader to choose his or her fate. Each page turn offers a choice, and based on the choice, you may continue in the story or be terminated.

Coville, Bruce, ed. *Bruce Coville's Book of Ghosts: Tales to Haunt You*. Scholastic. Illustrator: John Pierand. 160pp. Grades 5-8 🔲

These wildly popular titles include *Bruce Coville's Book of Ghosts, Bruce Coville's Book of*

Ghosts II, Bruce Coville's Book of Monsters, Bruce Coville's Book of Monsters II, Bruce Coville's Book of Nightmares, Bruce Coville's Book of Spine Tinglers, and *Bruce Coville's Book of Spine Tinglers II*. The collections are original stories written by Bruce Coville, Jane Yolen, and others.

Coville, Bruce. *Camp Haunted Hills*. Minstrel. Illustrator: John Pierard and Tom Newson. 100pp. Grades 3-5

Although only three titles have been published at this date, I believe these books were slated to become a series about a movie camp where anything can happen. Titles are *The Dinosaur that Followed Me Home, Some of My Best Friends Are Monsters*, and *How I Survived My Summer Vacation*.

Dadey, Debbie, and Marcia Jones. *Bailey City Monsters*. Scholastic. 80pp. Grades 2-5

Kids from the Bailey School fight evil in their neighborhood. There are nine titles to date, including *Vampire Trouble*.

Eeek! Stories to Make You Shriek. Various authors and illustrators. Grosset & Dunlap. 48pp. Grades 2-4

These quality books that sport scary stories are perfect for beginning readers. In an easy-to-read format, the stories are printed with large type and simple sentences. Illustrators include Brian Karas and Blanche Sims. Some titles include *Creep Show, Spooky Sleepover, Dragon Breath*, and *Haunted Bike*.

Eerie Indiana. Various authors and illustrators. William Morrow. 140pp. Grades 4-6

This mild series is set in the town of Eerie, Indiana. Simon, Marshall, Mitchell, and others live their daily life with spurts of weirdness and adventure, usually involving something supernatural.

Ellis, Carol. *Zodiac Chillers*. Random House. 170pp. Grades 6-8

Teens die under mysterious circumstances based upon birth dates and zodiac signs. Each title includes a different sign, for example, *Rage of Aquarius* and *Twisted Taurus*.

Flood, E. L. *Welcome Inn*. Troll. 142pp. Grades 4-6

In the guest house on Blackberry Island, young sleuths Molly and Gwen solve mysteries while encountering the supernatural. Titles include *Secret in the Moonlight* and *Ghost of a Chance*.

Fright Time: Spine Tingling Tales for Young Readers. Various authors. Baronet Books. 190pp. Grades 3-6

In each volume, you will find approximately three short stories. These stories are spiked with action and suspense. They are page-turners, but they are not realistic enough to cause nightmares.

Gave, Marc. *Fear Factory*. Price Stern Sloan. Illustrator: Scott Broxholm. 125pp. Grades 3-4

Eleven-year-old Bertram Potter and his grandfather, Poppa, have adventures in their wax museum. These stories are more fantasy and adventure than frightening, but they do involve the supernatural.

Hayes, Geoffry. *Graveyard Creeper Mysteries*. Random House. Illustrated by the author. 70pp. Grades 2-4

These first stepping-stone books involve two cute green monsters, Otto and Olivia, and their mysterious capers with supernatural beings.

Haynes, Betsy. *Bone Chillers*. HarperPaperbacks. 150pp. Grades 3-4

In these books, children are involved in dramatic stories. Titles include *Little Pet Shop of Horrors* and *blowtorch@psycho.com*. *Bone Chillers* has become a TV series as well.

Ingram, Scott, Q. L. Pearce, and R. C. Welch. *Scary Stories for Stormy Nights*. Lowell. Various illustrators. 90-125pp. Grades 5-7

The *Stormy Night* series is similar to the other collection by authors Pearce and Welch (*Scary Stories for Sleep-Overs*). The stories pack a punch for thrills and chills, delivering mutant werewolves, deadly wishes, and alien monsters. They are shocking, scary, and enjoyable for reluctant readers.

Kehret, Peg. *Frightmares*. Minstrel, 125pp. Grades 3-5 📼

This is one of the better choices for a series. Care Club members (Rosie and Kayo) solve cases and thwart evil. The level is a step up from Encyclopedia Brown, with common usage of the supernatural. Some titles include *Backstage Fright* and *The Ghost Followed Us Home*.

Lisle, Janet Taylor. *Investigators of the Unknown*. Orchard. 120pp. Grades 3-5

In this series, two books deal with spirits and the supernatural. In *Looking for Juliette*, Juliette the cat is missing, and the investigators use a Ouija board. *A Message from the Match Girl* is a story of a boy named Mike who believes that his dead mother is sending him messages via ghostly form.

Lubar, David. *Accidental Monsters*. Scholastic. 144pp. Grades 3-6

This is a series in which ordinary kids become monsters with funny results. Some titles include *Gloomy Ghost* and *Monster Road*.

Maccarone, Grace. *Monster Math*. Scholastic Math Readers. Illustrator: Marge Hartelius. Grades K-2

The *Hello Math* series is designed to teach children basic math concepts using math activities by Marilyn Burns. The titles at Level 1 include *Monster Math*, *Monster Math Picnic*, *Monster Math School Time*, and *Monster Money*.

Mueller, Virginia. *The Monster Books*. Albert Whitman. Illustrator: Lynn Munsinger. Kindergarten

These easy picture books feature Monster, a cute little green critter with monster friends and monster happenings. Monster is featured in *A Halloween Mask for Monster, Monster and the Baby, Monster Can't Sleep, Monster Goes to School, A Playhouse for Monster*, and *Monster's Birthday Hiccups*.

Murphy, Jill. *The Worst Witch*. Viking. Illustrated by the author. 100pp. Grades 3-4

In Miss Cackle's Academy for witches, Mildred just can't get things right. This is part of a series that includes *The Worst Witch, A Bad Spell for the Worst Witch, The Worst Witch at Sea*, and *The Worst Witch Strikes Again*.

Naylor, Phyllis Reynolds. *The Witch Books*. Delacorte. Illustrator: Joe Burleson. 179pp. Grades 5-8

Titles in this collection include *Witch Water, The Witch Herself, Witch's Sister*, and *The Witch's Eye*. In each story, Lynn and her family are brought to the brink of catastrophe due to the workings of a witch next door. The witch's power is insidious and seeps into the family. Each person is nearly destroyed as Lynn struggles to fight the evil power. These are more sophisticated stories, with fine writing and true character development not typical in most series.

Parker, Daniel. *Baby-sitter's Nightmares*. HarperPaperbacks. 160pp. Grades 6-8

In stories such as *Alone in the Dark*, baby-sitters undergo life threats and terror while trying to do their job.

Pearce, Q. L. and R. C. Welch. *Scary Stories for Sleep-Overs*. Price, Stern, Sloan. Various illustrators. 128pp. Grades 5-7

Believe the titles; these seven books (*More Scary, Still More Scary, Super Scary*, and so on) do have frightening stories in them. The stories typically involve science fiction elements (jungle plants that come to life, deadly robots, time travel that goes wrong) and teenagers who mysteriously find themselves in dangerous situations.

Pike, Christopher. *Spooksville*. Minstrel. 110pp. Grades 4-6

Included are more than 20 stories in which a gang of kids, living in a dangerous town, take on evil in every form. Try *The Hidden Beast* or *The Deadly Past* for a scare.

Pinkwater, Daniel. *The Werewolf Club*. Atheneum. Illustrator: Jill Pinkwater. 77pp. Grades 3-5

At the time of this writing, the first in the series, *The Magic Pretzel*, has been published. It is the only book I've ever read that begins with "Chapter (One) Minus Three." Typical of Pinkwater's style, it is very silly humor involving children who want to form a club of were-wolves.

Razzi, Jim. *Horror Show Series*. Troll. 92pp. Grades 3-5

Jim Razzi has written scary stories for a few publishing houses, and they typically have the same format. There are three short stories suitable for younger readers. Look for *Terror in the Mirror and Other Stories* and *The Haunted Playground.*

Regan, Dian Curtis. *Ghost Twins*. Scholastic. 109pp. Grades 3-5

Ghosts of twins and their dog, all drowned in a boating accident, solve mysteries with the aid of renters who stay at Kickingbird Lake. Titles include *The Mystery of the Disappearing Dogs* and *The Mystery of One Wish Pond.*

R. L. Stine's Ghosts of Fear Street. Various authors. Scholastic. 125pp. Grades 2-5

These were created to satisfy the younger siblings of teenagers purchasing the *Fear Street* series.

San Souci, Robert. *Short and Shivery*. Illustrators: Katherine Coville and Jaqueline Rogers. Grade 4 & Up 🔊

For those readers who want more after reading Schwartz's *Scary Stories*, this set includes four stories (*Short & Shivery, More Short & Shivery, Even More Short & Shivery*, and *A Terrifying Taste of Short & Shivery*). San Souci tells many of the same tales, but his writing is more elaborate. The stories are international in scope, and source notes are included. They have all been well reviewed and make great read-alouds.

Saunders, Susan. *The Black Cat Club*. HarperTrophy. Illustrator: Jane Manning. 90pp. Grades 2-4

Five children, one of whom is a ghost, form a club to solve mysteries and explore ghostly haunts. The plots are straightforward, and the ghost has a fondness for chocolate.

Stine, R. L. *Give Yourself Goosebumps*. Scholastic. 125pp.

Who can explain why we need to give ourselves goosebumps? I think we've had enough without adding to the frenzy, but R. L. Stine has inundated us with this series in the "choose your own" style.

Stine, R. L. *Goosebumps*. Scholastic. 125pp. Grades 2-5

This first published and wildly popular series needs no introduction. The writing quality is not excellent, but with titles like *The Blob That Ate Everyone*, what kid wouldn't take a look?

Stine, R. L. *Goosebumps Series 2000*. Scholastic. 125pp. Grades 2-5

This new series of Goosebumps was created for the new millennium. Perhaps the scariest aspect of this series is that as of September 2000, there already were 25 titles published.

Stone, Tom. *Graveyard School*. Bantam. 120pp. Grades 3-5 🔊

This series includes 17 titles set in a haunted school full of scared students. An activity (Mad-Lib level) follows each story, and some titles include *Boo Year's Eve* and *Tragic School Bus.*

Strickland, Brad. *John Bellair's Johnny Dixon in the Hand of the Necromancer*. Dial. 168pp. Grades 5-7

Brad Strickland has taken the famous Johnny Dixon and Professor Childermass and placed them into novels that include *The Bell, the Book and the Spellbinder*, *The Wrath of the Grinning Ghost*, and *The Drum, the Doll and the Zombie*.

Ten-Minute Thrillers. Various authors and illustrators. Lowell House. 100pp. Grades 4-6

There are other *Thriller* books in which stories range from three to five minutes (*Three-Minute Thrillers, Five-Minute Thrillers*). Some are scarier than others, but most of them deal with courage, creepy places, and unnamed mutant pursuers.

Ury, Allan B. Scary *Mysteries for Sleep-Overs*. Price, Stern, Sloan. Illustrator: Mia Tavonatti. 125pp. Grades 5-7

These are not mysteries in the Sherlock Holmes sense; they are twisted tales of teenagers encountering horrific situations. There are four books in this series (*More Scary Mysteries, Still More Scary Mysteries*, and *Even More Scary Mysteries*), all similar to the books written by Q. L. Pearce and R. C. Welch.

Warriner, Holly. *Spell Casters*. Aladdin. 125pp. Grades 5-7

A witch, Lucinda, comes to live with Sally and the two have adventures that mere mortals cannot understand. Titles include *Witch at the Door* and *Full Moon Magic*.

Weyn, Suzanne. *The House of Horrors Series: TrophyChillers*. HarperTrophy. 125pp. Grades 4-6

Jeepers Creepers, Rest in Pieces and *My Brother, the Ghost* are part of a series that explains what happens in haunted houses. These books are well reviewed and more interesting than most series.

Zullo, Allan. *True Ghost Stories*. Troll. 120pp. Grades 3-6

In these books, children see what happens to *Haunted Athletes, Haunted Kids, Haunted Houses*, and more. Each book contains short stories, and the vocabulary is aimed for the high-interest, low-level audience.

Audiovisual Materials

Audio

Many of the titles here are unabridged books on tape. In addition to using materials from Recorded Books, I have found <www.booksontape.com> useful to order from other publishers. It has listings from Listening Library, Simon & Schuster, Random House, Bantam Doubleday, and Books on Tape.

Alcock, Vivien. *Ghostly Companions: A Feast of Chilling Tales*. Listening Library, 1988. 3 cassettes. 3 hours. Grades 5-8
    These are thoughtful but not horrific tales.

Avi. *Something Upstairs: A Tale of Ghosts*. Recorded Books, 1992. 3 cassettes. 3.25 hours. Grades 4-7
    A boy must save a black slave from murder by traveling back in time.

Bellairs, John. *The Ghost in the Mirror*. Recorded Books, 1994. 3 cassettes. 4.25 hours. Grades 5-8
    A time-travel ghost story of Rose Rita and Mrs. Zimmerman.

Bellairs, John. *The House With a Clock In Its Walls*. Recorded Books, 1992. 3 cassettes. 4.5 hours. Grades 5-8
    When a boy goes to visit his magician uncle, they discover a hidden clock ticking off hours until doomsday.

Brown, Roberta Simpson. *The Scariest Stories Ever*. August House, 1992. 1 cassette. 60 minutes. Grades 6-8
    Some of the author's collected original stories are included.
    1. Lockers: Children are terrified in school.
    2. Fish Bait: A boy is doomed to a grisly fate when he catches Old Whiskers.

Byars, Betsy. *McMummy*. Recorded Books, 1995. 2 cassettes. 3 hours. Grades 2-5
    Mozie discovers a humming, human-sized pod in a greenhouse and believes it is a mummy.

Bruce Coville's Book of Monsters: Tales to Give You the Creeps. Listening Library, 1996. Unabridged. 2 cassettes. 1.25 hours. Grades 5-8
    This collection of stories read by the authors includes works by Bruce Coville and Jane Yolen.

Chiller. Erich Kunzel/Cincinnati Pops Orchestras. Telarc, 1989. 1 CD, 60 minutes. All ages.
    This is a combination of digital synthesizer sound effects and orchestral selections that range from *Phantom of the Opera* to Hitchcock's *Psycho*.

Cole, Joanna. *Bony-Legs*. Scholastic Records, 1984. 1 cassette. 17 minutes. Grades 1-3
    When a terrible witch vows to eat her for supper, a little girl escapes with the help of a mirror and comb given to her by the witch's dog and cat.

Cooper, Susan. *The Boggart*. Listening Library, 1997. 4 cassettes. 3.5 hours. Grades 4-8
    The spirit of a transported ghost causes mischief for a family.

Cooper, Susan. *The Boggart and the Monster*. Listening Library, 1998. 3 cassettes. 3.75 hours. Grades 4-8
    The family's spirit friend needs to help its cousin in Loch Ness.

Cooper, Susan. *The Boggart Set*. Books on Tape, 1997. 7 cassettes. 8.5 hours. Grades 4-8
    The two stories of Susan Cooper are combined as a set.

Coville, Bruce. *The Ghost in the Big Brass Bed*. Recorded Books, 1996. 4 cassettes. 4.75 hours. Grades 3-5
    Nina and her friend Chris solve the mystery of the antique shop with the aid of the ancient ghost.

Coville, Bruce. *The Ghost in the Third Row*. Recorded Books, 1996. 3 cassettes. 3.25 hours. Grades 3-5
    Nina and Chris solve the mystery and stop the haunting of a ghost in a theater company.

Coville, Bruce. *The Ghost Wore Gray*. Recorded Books, 1993. 3 cassettes. 4 hours. Grades 3-5
    When Nina and Chris spend time at a bed and breakfast, the ghost of a Confederate soldier brings excitement and history to this mystery.

Coville, Bruce. *The Monster's Ring*. Recorded Books, 1992. 2 cassettes. 2.25 hours. Grades 3-5
    Russell Crannaker buys a "Monster's Ring" in a magic shop and turns into a hairy beast.

Creech, Sharon. *Pleasing the Ghost*. Recorded Books, 1999. 1 cassette. 1.5 hours. Grades 2-4
    After his dad dies, Dennis can see ghosts. When the ghost of Uncle Arvey comes along, he teams with Dennis to finish some business.

Dahl, Roald. *The Witches*. Recorded Books, 1994. 5 CDs or 4 cassettes. 5 hours. Grades 3-6
    A favorite of children, this story brings a boy face to face with real witches who would like to turn him into a mouse.

Delton, Judy. *Camp Ghost-Away*. Recorded Books, 1997. 1 cassette. 45 minutes. Grades 2-4
    The Pee Wee Scouts are in for a scare one night while camping.

Dickens, Charles. *A Christmas Carol*. Recorded Books, 1980. 2 cassettes, or 2 CDs. 3 hours.
The ghosts of Christmas haunt Scrooge in this unabridged reading of a classic.

Fleishman, Sid. *The 13th Floor: A Ghost Story*. Listening Library, 1995. 2 cassettes. 2 hours. Grades 3-5
When he travels back in time, Buddy saves his sister from a hanging and meets a pirate relative.

Fleishman, Sid. *The Ghost in the Noonday Sun*. Recorded Books, 1993. 3 cassettes. 4.25 hours. Grades 3-5
This is a great story of ghosts, shipwrecks and pirates.

Halloween Fun. Kimbo®, 1989. 1 cassette. 40 minutes. Kindergarten
These fun songs for the very young are not too scary.

Halloween Havoc. K-Tel, 1996. 1 cassette. 1 hour. N/A
There are very few materials that I would NOT recommend, but the second story on this tape, "The Dark-Net," is so bad that I doubt any parent or teacher would want children to listen to it. When I shut it off, demons were convincing a boy that he had been chosen to become one of them, but first he had to murder someone.

The Hits of Halloween: Creepy Classics, Scary Effects and A Chilling Ghost Story. Intersound Inc., 1994. 1 CD. 35 minutes. Grades 3-5
Included on this CD are "The Tell-Tale Heart" and a medley of creepy songs, including "A Night on Bald Mountain" and "The Tempest."
Reviews not available.

Hobbs, Will. *Ghost Canoe*. Random House, 1999. 4 cassettes. 6 hours. Grades 5-8
Nathan finds himself in a mysterious situation when a stranger comes to town looking for treasure.

Holt, David. *Mostly Ghostly Stories*. High Windy Audio, 1990. 1 cassette. 1 hour. Grades 1-6
Using his folk style, this storyteller/musician uses music to accompany scary stories, such as "Dead Aaron Kelly."

Holt, David. *Tailybone*. High Windy Audio, 1987. 1 cassette. 40 minutes. Grades 4-6
   1. Ross and Anna: A man builds his cabin on a stone with a hole in the center. When he makes his first cooking fire, the heat draws out the hibernating rattlesnakes from below, and…well, you can guess the rest.

Howe, Deborah. *Bunnicula*. Listening Library, 2000. 2 cassettes. 2 hours. Grades 3-5
Part bunny, part juice-sucking vampire, Bunnicula frightens the animals at the Monroe house.

Howe, James. *The Celery Stalks at Midnight*. Listening Library, 2000. 2 cassettes. 1.5 hours. Grades 3-5

When Bunnicula disappears, Howie, Harold, and Chester track him down.

Howe, James. *Nighty-Nightmare*. Listening Library, 2000. 2 cassettes. 1.5 hours. Grades 3-5

Animals take action when they hear scary sounds at the Monroe campsite.

Irving, Washington. *Glenn Close Reads the Legend of Sleepy Hollow*. Sony, Rabbit Ears, 1989. 1 cassette. 30 minutes. Grades 3-6

This is the story of Ichabod Crane and the Headless Horseman, abridged and told with spooky music. I highly recommend both the audio and video versions narrated by Glenn Close.

Jacques, Brian. *Seven Strange and Ghostly Tales*. Listening Library, 1996. 3 cassettes. 4.4 hours. Grades 4-7

Read by Brian Jacques, these seven tales involve suspense and the supernatural.

Kehret, Peg. *The Frightmares Series*. Recorded Books, 1996-1997. Each book is 2 cassettes. 3 hours.

Eight of Peg Kehret's stories, full of mystery and suspense, are included.

Krensky, Stephen. *Fraidy Cats*. Scholastic Cassettes, 1993. 1 cassette and read-along book. 5 minutes. Grades K-2

Two cats imagine great horrors while readying for bed.

Levitt, Marc Joel. *Tales of an October Moon: Haunting Stories from New England*. North Star Records, August House 1989. 1 hour. Grades 3-6

These shivery tales are wonderfully told.

1. The Scituate Reservoir: This is the story of the flooding of towns near Providence, Rhode Island and one man's curse on the reservoir project.

Lieberman, Syd. *The Tell-Tale Heart and Other Terrifying Tales*. Studiomedia, 1991. 1 cassette. 47 minutes. Grades 6-8

It takes great courage to record such classics as these, but they are powerful and energetic retellings, with eerie music. The Poe tales are perfect, but also try:

1. The Pardoner's Tale: Three men meet Death in a twisted tale of treachery.

One Scary Night: Thirty Haunting Halloween Tales. Read by Clive Revill and Paddi Edwards. Poet Tree, 1993. 1 cassette and read-along book, 50 minutes. Grades 5-8

This collection of poetry is accompanied by eerie music and spooky sound effects—perfect for sharing around Halloween.

1. The Raven: This is one of the finest recitations of this classic tale.
2. The Hell-Bound Train: If you don't mend your ways after listening to this, there's no hope for you.

Prelutsky, Jack. *Nightmares and The Headless Horseman Rides Tonight: Poems to Trouble Your Sleep.* HarperCollins, 1983. 1 cassette. 40 minutes. Grades 4-6

These poems are performed by the author and include spooky music.

Reneaux, J. J. *Cajun Ghost Stories.* August House, 1992. 1 cassette. 68 minutes. Grades 3-6

Six Cajun ghost stories, told by the author, are spiced with swamp creatures and villains. Audio only, no print version.

Rix, Jamie. *Ghostly Tales for Ghastly Kids.* Chivers Audio Books, 1995. 3 cassettes. 3.5 hours. Grades 4-7

These 15 unabridged stories are lengthy, but well narrated by Andrew Sachs. Using different voices to portray characters, his efforts make the best of difficult reading.

San Souci, Robert. *Even More Short & Shivery: Thirty Spine-Tingling Tales.* Recorded Books, 1997. 3 cassettes. 4 hours. Grades 4-6

Included are all of the stories in the book, told by various narrators.

San Souci, Robert. *Short & Shivery: Thirty Chilling Tales.* Recorded Books, 1994. 4 cassettes. 5 hours. Grades 4-6

Mark Hammer adds an eerie chill as he narrates these folktales collected from many countries.

San Souci, Robert. *More Short & Shivery: Thirty Terrifying Tales.* Recorded Books, 1995. 4 cassettes. 5 hours. Grades 4-6

Mark Hammer reads these tales with skill and style.

Scary Halloween. Creative Music Marketing, 1996. 1 CD, 21 minutes. Grade 4 & Up

These are truly scary sound effects, including "Cruel Chase" and "Virtual Grave." Beware; the anticipation is terrifying!

Schwartz, Alvin. *Scary Stories 3.* HarperCollins, 1991. 1 cassette. 80 minutes.

These short stories and songs are performed by George S. Irving, who has the ability to make even the scariest story seem like fun…at the time.

Schwartz, Alvin. *Scary Stories to Tell in the Dark.* HarperCollins, 1987. 1 cassette. 41 minutes.

George S. Irving can take the creepiest story and make it fun. This is a great recording of a well-loved book.

Silverman, Erica. *Big Pumpkin.* Recorded Books, 1998. 1 cassette. 15 minutes. Grades K-3

The old witch needs help removing the biggest pumpkin from her vine. A monster, bat, and vampire help her and are rewarded with pumpkin pie.

Simon, Seymour. *The Halloween Horror and Other Cases*. Recorded Books, 2000. 1 cassette. 75 minutes.

Sixth-grade sleuth Einstein Anderson uses his scientific knowledge to solve a variety of problems, including getting rid of a bully and preserving a snow sculpture.

Spooky Classics for Children. Narrated by Jim Weiss. Greathall Productions, 1997. 40 minutes. Grades 3-6

Three classics are included: *The Canterville Ghost*, *Dr. Heidegger's Experiment*, and *The Sending of Dana Da*.

Stone, Tom B. *The Graveyard School Series*. Recorded Books, 1997. Each book is 2 cassettes. 2.5 hours. Grades 4-6

Spooky danger and grisly humor exist in a school where students are dying to go to class.

Torrence, Jackie. *Jump Tales*. Rounder Records, 1991. 1 cassette. 40 minutes. Grades 1-5

If you haven't heard Jackie tell a tale, you're missing some of the best interpretations of story. These fully developed jump tales draw in the listener.
1. Lavender: This is a great version of the vanishing hitchhiker, similar to the version in San Souci's *Short and Shivery* collection.
2. The Yellow Ribbon: When she takes the ribbon off, her head falls off.

Torrence, Jackie. *Tales for Scary Times*. Ear Wig Music Company, 1985. 1 cassette. 40 minutes. Grades 2-6

Jackie Torrence is a great storyteller, and the classic story "The Golden Arm" is her trademark. If you never have the opportunity to hear her live, try this tape. You'll hear why she's become a legend in her own time.

Westall, Robert. *The Stones of Muncaster Cathedral*. Recorded Books, 1994. 2 cassettes. 3 hours. Grades 5-8

A stone gargoyle has hideous powers as discovered by Joe Clark, a steeplejack.

Young, Richard, and Judy Dockrey Young. *Favorite Scary Stories of American Children*. 2 cassettes (one per age range). 40 minutes each. Grades K-3, Grades 4-6

These spooky stories are well known to children. Each cassette is age appropriate.

Young, Richard, and Judy Dockrey Young. *Ghost Stories from the American Southwest*. August House. Grades 6-8

These stories are told by master storytellers, and they're frightening enough to chill the listener to the bone.

Young, Richard, and Judy Dockrey Young. *The Head on the High Road: Ghost Stories from the Southwest*. August House. 1 cassette. 60 minutes. Grades 3-6

These are milder stories, enhanced with music and sound effects, found in audio version only.

Video

Arthur's Scary Stories. Random House Home Video, 2000. 1 videocassette. 45 minutes. Animated. Grades K-2

This video contains two episodes from the television program by Marc Brown.

DeFelice, Cynthia. *The Dancing Skeleton*. American School Publishers, 1991. 1 videocassette. 15 minutes. Illustrated by Robert Andrew Parker. Iconographic. Grades K-4

This is an iconographic version of Aaron Kelly, the dead man who wants to dance.

Dickens, Charles. *Ghost Stories*. Celebrity Home Entertainment, 1989. 1 videocassette. 60 minutes. Animated. Grades 3-8

Selected from Charles Dickens' *Pickwick Papers*, this trio of chilling tales is brought to life through animation.

Franklin in the Dark. USA Home Entertainment, 2000. 1 videocassette. 25 minutes. Animated. Grades K-2

When Franklin's parents discover he's afraid of small dark places, Mrs. Turtle tells him the story to assuage his fears.

Irving, Washington. *Legend of Sleepy Hollow*. Narrated by Glenn Close. Sony, Rabbit Ears, 1988. 1 videocassette. 30 min. Iconographic. Grades 3-6

Dramatic sound effects and some animation help create this excellent version of the *Legend of Sleep Hollow*.

Little Witch. Based on the books by Deborah Hautzig. Sony Wonder, 1999. 1 videocassette. 30 minutes. Grades K-2

The *Little Witch* books are presented with music and animation.

Monster Mash. Universal Studios Home Video, 1999. 1 videocassette. 64 minutes. Grades K-3

Frank, Wolf, and Drac are about to be thrown out of the Ghoul Guild unless they can master one last challenge—frighten a "typical" human family.

Scary Stories: Terrifying Tales Traditionally Told. Atlas Video, 1991. 35 minutes. Live storytelling. Grades 1-4

Four storytellers (Joe Bruchac, Olga Loya, Alice McGill, and Jon Spelman) tell spooky stories to an audience of school-aged listeners. Stories include "Chebai—An Adirondack Ghost Story," "A Light at Night," "Taily Po," and "The Flying Skeleton."

Scary Tales: The Teller and the Tale. Comtel Productions, 1986. 1 videocassette. 30 minutes. Live storytelling. Grades 1-4

Jackie Torrence and her friends bring to life five stories, including "Wiley and the Hairy Man" and "The Golden Arm."

Schultz, Charles. *It's the Great Pumpkin, Charlie Brown.* Peanuts Home Video Library, 1994. 1 videocassette. 30 minutes. Illustrated by the author. Animated. Grades K-3

On Halloween, the Peanuts gang tells the legend of a giant pumpkin.

Slightly Scary Stories for Halloween. Weston Woods, 1999. Animated. 1 videocassette. 29 minutes. Grades 1-3

Included are three stories—*By the Light of the Halloween Moon, What's Under My Bed?,* and *Teeny-Tiny and the Witch-Woman.* The last story is scary, but the first two are not.

Stevenson, James. *What's Under My Bed?* Weston Woods, 1989. 1 videocassette. 8 minutes. Animated. Illustrated by the author. Grades K-2

When his grandchildren can't sleep, Grandpa tells about his own childhood and the bedtime fears he experienced. There are good sound effects for students to express. This story also can be found in *Slightly Scary Stories for Halloween,* by Weston Woods, 1999.

Stutson, Caroline. *By the Light of the Halloween Moon.* Weston Woods, 1995. Animated with illustrations by Kevin Hawke. 1 videocassette. Grades K-2

In a fun, cumulative tale with spooky illustrations, a girl attracts hungry listeners while playing her violin. Also found in *Slightly Scary Stories for Halloween,* by Weston Woods, 1999.

Teeny-Tiny and the Witch-Woman and Other Scary Stories. Weston Woods, 1985. 1 videocassette. 38 minutes. Animated. Grades 1-3

Stories included are "Teeny-Tiny and the Witch-Woman" by Barbara Walker, "The King of Cats" by Paul Galdone, and "A Dark, Dark Tale" by Ruth Brown.

Walker, Barbara. *Teeny-Tiny and the Witch Woman.* Weston Woods, 1979. Also found in *Slightly Scary Stories for Halloween,* by Weston Woods, 1999. Animated with illustrations by Michael Foreman. Grades 2-4

This is a scary Hansel and Gretel-type story; the Turkish version portrays a knife-wielding witch and three brothers.

Web Sites

The Case.Com for Kids
<www.thecase.com/kids/>
This free site has mysteries to solve, scary stories, magic tricks and contests. The stories are mild, and they load quickly—a plus when dealing with children. Grades 2-5

E-Cards: Halloween Cards
<www.e-cards.com/group/halloween/>
This site allows users to create and send cards. There also is a section for pumpkin contests, an interactive ghost story, and other safe, fun Halloween treats. Grades 1-3

Find a Grave Site
This site is devoted to cataloging the locations of graves of famous people. There are many actual tombstones. Users can search by name, location, claim to fame, and dates of birth or death.
Grade 5 & Up

Grave of Myles Standish
This picture appears courtesy of *Robert Rich*

Folklore and Mythology Electronic Texts
<www.pitt.edu/~dash/folktexts.html>
This research site is devoted to cataloging thousands of tales by alphabetical topics and Aarne-Thompson folktale motif. Grades 4-6

Some scary stories can be found at:

<www.pitt.edu/%7Edash/type0779.html>
It includes the story "A Hand from the Grave" in which wayward children's hands, after death, refuse to stay buried.

<www.pitt.edu/%7Edash/type4025.html>
The story is exactly what it says: "Haunted by the ghost of a murdered child."

<www.pitt.edu/%7Edash/type0780.html>
Singing Bones: This site includes tales about murder victims whose body parts literally sing out for justice.

<www.pitt.edu/%7Edash/vampire.html>
Vampire and ghost stories from Russia

<www.pitt.edu/%7Edash/werewolf.html>
Werewolf legends from Germany

Heather's Scary Halloween Page
<www.heathersholidaze.com/hallo/todo.html>
This informative site includes pictures, tips for safe trick-or-treating, and a coloring page.
Grades 1-3

The Internet Public Library Story Hour
<www.ipl.org/youth/StoryHour/>
This section features folktales, which are illustrated. Some, but not all, have scary themes. They are mild enough to use with the intermediate-aged students, but interesting enough for the upper grades as well. Grades 3-6

The Moonlit Road

Not for the faint of heart, this is one scary site! This award-winning Web site contains ghost stories and strange stories of the American South, told by the region's most celebrated storytellers. Both text and streaming audio versions are available, with notes and discussion sections. Grade 5 & Up with online warning for younger audiences.

The Perpetual Preschool Halloween Art
<www.perpetualpreschool.com/halloweenart.html>
The Perpetual Preschool is a massive site, and the Halloween section is just one of many branches. It contains quick and simple games, snacks, songs, and art activities submitted by users. Perfect for preschool or story hours. Grades K-2

Scary.com IS Halloween
All kinds of scary stuff are included at this site, along with tons of flash movies, sounds, stories, and games. You need a little patience for the images to load, but it's lots of fun.
Grades 4-6

Scary Halloween Sounds
<www.superglobe.com/halloween.htm>
Fun! Midi sounds. All ages.

Further Reading

Scary Stories and Storytelling

Barchers, Suzanne. *Scary Readers Theatre*. Teacher Ideas Press, 1994. Illustrator: Joan Garner. 155pp.

Readers Theater is the art of using books in a dramatic style, either in play production or other performance art. This book simply narrows the genre to scary stories, and contains folktales, urban legends, ghost stories and myths, with narration and parts to be performed.

Justice, Jennifer, ed. *The Ghost and I: Scary Stories for Participatory Telling*. Yellow Moon Press, 1992.

This is a collection of short stories written to tell. It is divided into age-appropriate sections, with five or six stories for each level (Pre-K through junior high). Each story is printed with a step-by-step performance technique guide.

Koerner, Julie. *More Scary Story Starters*. Lowell House, 1997. Illustrator: Kerry Manwaring.

This book of activities and illustrations is designed to spark imaginative writing. Some exercises include making creepy comparisons, using scary similes, using pictures to spark a story, and writing an ending to complete a story.

MacDonald, Margaret Read. *When the Lights Go Out: Twenty Scary Tales to Tell*. H. W. Wilson, 1988.

If you have never dared to tell a scary story and would like some practical tips, this is the place to start. It is a great resource that includes traditional tales, folktales, and the famous "Witches' Brew." MacDonald gives ethno-poetic interpretations (technique guides) for each story.

Censorship

Web site:
Controversial Children's Books and The Social Studies
<www.iac.net/~pfilio/ahern.htm>

This site discusses censorship in children's literature. One section includes important references to folklore titles, such as *Scary Stories to Tell in the Dark*.

Booktalks, Presenting Children's Literature, and General Selection Aids

Bauer, Caroline Feller. *This Way to Books*. H. W. Wilson, 1983. Illustrated by Lynn Gates.

A resource that now is becoming dated, this book contains ideas to use with children's books and book-related activities.

Brodart, Joni. *Booktalk! Booktalking and School Visiting for Young Adult Audiences.* H. W. Wilson. 1980.

This title, along with the series of *Booktalk!* titles, will help you in your strategies to promote novels. As of this writing, there are five titles, all published by H. W. Wilson.

Freeman, Judy. *Books Kids Will Sit Still For: The Complete Read-Aloud Guide.* Bowker, 1990.

This book and its follow-up, *More Books Kids Will Sit Still For*, contain annotations for tried and true stories. Short activities also are included, with related book titles for many entries.

Herald, Diana. *Genreflecting: A Guide to Reading Interests in Genre Fiction, 4th ed.* Libraries Unlimited, 1995.

This selection aid covers books and media for upper-level students. Each chapter is devoted to a specific genre, horror included, with subgenre listings and relevant titles. Resources for further research are included.

Rochman, Hazel. *Tales of Love and Terror.* American Library Association, 1987.

A book that teaches the art of the booktalk and offers practical approaches to booktalking classics. There also is a video available from the ALA.

Spencer, Pam, and Janis Ansell. *What Do Children Read Next? A Reader's Guide to Fiction for Children.* Volume 2. Gale, 1997.

This resource lists 1,600 titles of books for K-8 readers. Each entry includes a summary, related themes, other books to enjoy, and reviews.

Appendix A

Selection Policy:

The best resource for any challenge assistance or encouragement is:

The Office for Intellectual Freedom of the American Library Association
50 East Huron Street
Chicago, IL 60611
312-280-4223
<www.ala.org/oif.html>

If you would like a book outlining its beliefs, you may find this title of use:

Intellectual Freedom Manual, fifth edition, Chicago: ALA, Office for Intellectual Freedom, 1996.

In my search for collection development policies, I discovered these helpful sites:

American Library Association's Workbook for Selection Policy Writing
<www.eff.org/pub/CAF/books/ala.selection>
The ALA is the authority on the topic of selection policy. Use this site's format to write your own policy. It is complete with sample letters to use for challenged materials.

Patchwork: Handbook for Montana's Small School Libraries
<www.lib.wmc.edu/pub/patchwork/collection.html>
If you want to look at other school library selection policies, or if you want a policy specifically written for school library needs, try this site. It includes tips on collection development by Mary Bushing, coordinator for the libraries.

MGPL Webrary
<www.webrary.org/inside/colldevtoc.html>
This is the most thorough collection development and materials selection policy I have come across. It includes a community description, mission statement, selection policy, *The Library Bill of Rights*, and collection sub-headings for each department (i.e., Adult Fiction, Audiovisual).

Appendix B

Addresses for Ordering Information

The William Forgey *Campfire Tales* books:
ISC Books, Inc.
1370 East 86th Place
Merrillville, IN 46410
1-800-541-7323

Scary Reader's Theater:
Teacher Ideas Press
PO Box 6633
Englewood, NJ
1-800-237-6124

Audio Production/Distribution:
American School Publishers
c/o SRA McGraw Hill
1-800-843-8855

Greathall Productions
PO Box 813
Benicia, CA 94510
1-800-477-6234

High Windy Audio
c/o August House Publishers
Box 3223
Little Rock, AR 72203

Intersound Inc.
PO Box 1724
Roswell, GA 30077

Subject Index

Title Index

Author Index

About the Author

Pamela Schembri grew up listening to her father tell stories—some from his immigrant childhood in the Bronx, others from his wily imagination. Spellbound, she was transported to wherever his words took her. Later, when Ms. Schembri became a school library media specialist, she found the powerful tool of storytelling essential in her library program. Scary stories seemed to spark the most vociferous reactions and increased the children's interest in reading. Their demand never ceased, so she feverishly researched to maintain a steady supply of quality books. *Using Scary Stories in the Classroom* is the result of eight years of her work. Now, as an invited guest to conferences, schools and libraries, Ms. Schembri shares not only these tales of terror but also the full range of stories she has written and collected through her professional career. She and her daughter live north of New York City, where she is a part-time school media specialist in the Pine Bush Central School District.